Juan Ponce de León

and His Lands of Discovery

Juan Ponce de León
and His Lands of Discovery

John C. Davenport

Series Consulting Editor **William H. Goetzmann**
Jack S. Blanton, Sr. Chair in History and American Studies
University of Texas, Austin

CHELSEA HOUSE
PUBLISHERS
A Haights Cross Communications ✦ Company ®
Philadelphia

CHELSEA HOUSE PUBLISHERS
VP, NEW PRODUCT DEVELOPMENT Sally Cheney
DIRECTOR OF PRODUCTION Kim Shinners
CREATIVE MANAGER Takeshi Takahashi
MANUFACTURING MANAGER Diann Grasse

Staff for JUAN PONCE DE LEÓN
EXECUTIVE EDITOR Lee Marcott
EDITORIAL ASSISTANT Carla Greenberg
PRODUCTION EDITOR Noelle Nardone
PHOTO EDITOR Sarah Bloom
COVER AND INTERIOR DESIGNER Keith Trego
LAYOUT 21st Century Publishing and Communications, Inc.

A Haights Cross Communications ✦ Company ®

www.chelseahouse.com

First Printing

9 8 7 6 5 4 3 2 1

Library of Congress Cataloging-in-Publication Data applied for.

ISBN 0-7910-8607-0

All links and web addresses were checked and verified to be correct at the time of publication.
Because of the dynamic nature of the web, some addresses and links may have changed since
publication and may no longer be valid.

Table of Contents

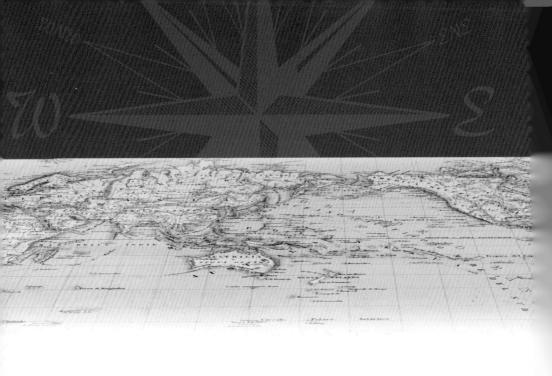

Introduction

by William H. Goetzmann
Jack S. Blanton, Sr. Chair in History and American Studies
University of Texas, Austin

Explorers have always been adventurers. They were, and still are, people of vision and most of all, people of curiosity. The English poet Rudyard Kipling once described the psychology behind the explorer's curiosity:

"Something hidden. Go and find it. Go and
      look behind the Ranges—
Something lost behind the Ranges. Lost and
      waiting for you. Go!" [1]

Miguel de Cervantes, the heroic author of *Don Quixote*, longed to be an explorer-conquistador. So he wrote a personal letter to King Phillip II of Spain asking to be appointed to lead an expedition to the New World. Phillip II turned down his request. Later, while in prison, Cervantes gained revenge. He wrote the immortal story of *Don Quixote*, a broken-down, half-crazy "Knight of La Mancha" who "explored" Spain with his faithful sidekick, Sancho Panza. His was perhaps the first of a long line of revenge novels—a lampoon of the real explorer-conquistadors.

Most of these explorer-conquistadors, such as Columbus and Cortés, are often regarded as heroes who discovered new worlds and empires. They were courageous, brave and clever, but most of them were also cruel to the native peoples they met. For example, Cortés, with a small band of 500 Spanish conquistadors, wiped out the vast

Aztec Empire. He insulted the Aztecs' gods and tore down their temples. A bit later, far down in South America, Francisco Pizarro and Hernando de Soto did the same to the Inca Empire, which was hidden behind a vast upland desert among Peru's towering mountains. Both tasks seem to be impossible, but these conquistadors not only overcame nature and savage armies, they stole their gold and became rich nobles. More astounding, they converted whole countries and even a continent to Spanish Catholicism. Cathedrals replaced blood-soaked temples, and the people of South and Central America, north to the Mexican border, soon spoke only two languages—Portuguese in Brazil and Spanish in the rest of the countries, even extending through the Southwest United States.

Most of the cathedral building and language changing has been attributed to the vast numbers of Spanish and Portuguese missionaries, but trade with and even enslavement of the natives must have played a great part. Also playing an important part were great missions that were half churches and half farming and ranching communities. They offered protection from enemies and a life of stability for the natives. Clearly vast numbers of natives took to these missions. The missions vied with the cruel native caciques, or rulers, for protection and for a constant food supply. We have to ask ourselves: Did the Spanish conquests raise the natives' standard of living? And did a religion of love appeal more to the natives than ones of sheer terror, where hearts were torn out and bodies were tossed down steep temple stairways as sacrifices that were probably eaten by dogs or other wild beasts? These questions are something to think about as you read the Explorers of New Lands series. They are profound questions even today.

"New Lands" does not only refer to the Western Hemisphere and the Spanish/Portuguese conquests there. Our series should probably begin with the fierce Vikings—Eric the Red, who discovered Greenland in 982, and Leif Ericson, who discovered North America in 1002, followed, probably a year later, by a settler named Bjorni. The Viking sagas (or tales passed down through generations) tell the stories of these men and of Fredis, the first woman discoverer of a New Land. She became a savior of the Viking men when, wielding a broadsword and screaming like a madwoman, she single-handedly routed the native Beothuks who were about to wipe out the earliest Viking settlement in North America that can be identified. The Vikings did not, however, last as long in North America as they did in Greenland and Northern England. The natives of the north were far tougher than the natives of the south and the Caribbean.

Far away, on virtually the other side of the world, traders were making their way east toward China. Persians and Arabs as well as Mongols established a trade route to the Far East via such fabled cities as Samarkand, Bukhara, and Kashgar and across the Hindu Kush and Pamir Mountains to Tibet and beyond. One of our volumes tells the story of Marco Polo, who crossed from Byzantium (later Constantinople) overland along the Silk Road to China and the court of Kublai Khan, the Mongol emperor. This was a crossing over wild deserts and towering mountains, as long as Columbus's Atlantic crossing to the Caribbean. His journey came under less dangerous (no pirates yet) and more comfortable conditions than that of the Polos, Nicolo and Maffeo, who from 1260 to 1269 made their way across these endless wastes while making friends, not enemies, of the fierce Mongols. In 1271, they took along Marco Polo (who was Nicolo's son and Maffeo's nephew). Marco became a great favorite of Kublai Khan and stayed in China till 1292. He even became the ruler of one of Kublai Khan's largest cities, Hangchow.

Before he returned, Marco Polo had learned of many of the Chinese ports, and because of Chinese trade to the west across the Indian Ocean, he knew of East Africa as far as Zanzibar. He also knew of the Spice Islands and Japan. When he returned to his home city of Venice he brought enviable new knowledge with him, about gunpowder, paper and paper money, coal, tea making, and the role of worms that create silk! While captured by Genoese forces, he dictated an account of his amazing adventures, which included vast amounts of new information, not only about China, but about the geography of nearly half of the globe. This is one hallmark of great explorers. How much did they contribute to the world's body of knowledge? These earlier inquisitive explorers were important members of a culture of science that stemmed from world trade and genuine curiosity. For the Polos crossing over deserts, mountains and very dangerous tribal-dominated countries or regions, theirs was a hard-won knowledge. As you read about Marco Polo's travels, try and count the many new things and descriptions he brought to Mediterranean countries.

Besides the Polos, however, there were many Islamic traders who traveled to China, like Ibn Battuta, who came from Morocco in Northwest Africa. An Italian Jewish rabbi-trader, Jacob d'Ancona, made his way via India in 1270 to the great Chinese trading port of Zaitun, where he spent much of his time. Both of these explorer-travelers left extensive reports of their expeditions, which rivaled those of the Polos but were less known, as are the neglected accounts of Roman Catholic friars who entered China, one of whom became bishop of Zaitun.[2]

In 1453, the Turkish Empire cut off the Silk Road to Asia. But Turkey was thwarted when, in 1497 and 1498, the Portuguese captain Vasco da Gama sailed from Lisbon around the tip of Africa, up to Arab-controlled Mozambique, and across the

Indian Ocean to Calicut on the western coast of India. He faced the hostility of Arab traders who virtually dominated Calicut. He took care of this problem on a second voyage in 1502 with 20 ships to safeguard the interests of colonists brought to India by another Portuguese captain, Pedro Álvares Cabral. Da Gama laid siege to Calicut and destroyed a fleet of 29 warships. He secured Calicut for the Portuguese settlers and opened a spice route to the islands of the Indies that made Portugal and Spain rich. Spices were valued nearly as much as gold since without refrigeration, foods would spoil. The spices disguised this, and also made the food taste good. Virtually every culture in the world has some kind of stew. Almost all of them depend on spices. Can you name some spices that come from the faraway Spice Islands?

Of course most Americans have heard of Christopher Columbus, who in 1492 sailed west across the Atlantic for the Indies and China. Instead, on four voyages, he reached Hispaniola (now Haiti and the Dominican Republic), Cuba and Jamaica. He created a vision of a New World, populated by what he misleadingly called Indians.

Conquistadors like the Italian sailing for Portugal, Amerigo Vespucci, followed Columbus and in 1502 reached South America at what is now Brazil. His landing there explains Brazil's Portuguese language origins as well as how America got its name on Renaissance charts drawn on vellum or dried sheepskin.

Meanwhile, the English heard of a Portuguese discovery of marvelous fishing grounds off Labrador (discovered by the Vikings and rediscovered by a mysterious freelance Portuguese sailor named the "Labrador"). They sent John Cabot in 1497 to locate these fishing grounds. He found them, and Newfoundland and Labrador as well. It marked the British discovery of North America.

In this first series there are strange tales of other explorers of new lands—Juan Ponce de León, who sought riches and possibly a fountain of youth (everlasting life) and died in Florida; Francisco Coronado, whose men discovered the Grand Canyon and at Zuñi established what became the heart of the Spanish Southwest before the creation of Santa Fe; and de Soto, who after helping to conquer the Incas, boldly ravaged what is now the

American South and Southeast. He also found that the Indian Mound Builder cultures, centered in Cahokia across the Mississippi from present-day St. Louis, had no gold and did not welcome him. Garcilaso de la Vega, the last Inca, lived to write de Soto's story, called *The Florida of the Inca*—a revenge story to match that of Cervantes, who like Garcilaso de la Vega ended up in the tiny Spanish town of Burgos. The two writers never met. Why was this—especially since Cervantes was the tax collector? Perhaps this was when he was in prison writing *Don Quixote*.

In 1513 Vasco Núñez de Balboa discovered the Pacific Ocean "from a peak in Darien"[3] and was soon beheaded by a rival conquistador. But perhaps the greatest Pacific feat was Ferdinand Magellan's voyage around the world from 1519 to 1522, which he did not survive.

Magellan was a Portuguese who sailed for Spain down the Atlantic and through the Strait of Magellan—a narrow passage to the Pacific. He journeyed across that ocean to the Philippines, where he was killed in a fight with the natives. As a recent biography put it, he had "sailed over the edge of the world."[4] His men continued west, and the *Victoria,* the last of his five ships, worn and battered, reached Spain.

Sir Francis Drake, a privateer and lifelong enemy of Spain, sailed for Queen Elizabeth of England on a secret mission in 1577 to find a passage across the Americas for England. Though he sailed, as he put it, "along the backside of Nueva Espanola"[5] as far north as Alaska perhaps, he found no such passage. He then sailed west around the world to England. He survived to help defeat the huge Spanish Armada sent by Phillip II to take England in 1588. Alas he could not give up his bad habit of privateering, and died of dysentery off Porto Bello, Panama. Drake did not find what he was looking for "beyond the ranges," but it wasn't his curiosity that killed him. He may have been the greatest explorer of them all!

While reading our series of great explorers, think about the many questions that arise in your reading, which I hope inspires you to great deeds.

Notes

1. Rudyard Kipling, "The Explorer" (1898). See Jon Heurtl, *Rudyard Kipling: Selected Poems* (New York: Barnes & Noble Books, 2004), 7.

2. Jacob D'Ancona, David Shelbourne, translator, *The City of Light: The Hidden Journal of the Man Who Entered China Four Years Before Marco Polo* (New York: Citadel Press, 1997).

3. John Keats, "On First Looking Into Chapman's Homer."

4. Laurence Bergreen, *Over the Edge of the World: Magellan's Terrifying Circumnavigation of the Globe* (New York: William Morrow & Company, 2003).

5. See Richard Hakluyt, *Principal Navigations, Voyages, Traffiques and Discoveries of the English Nation*; section on Sir Francis Drake.

1

1493

This fleet was larger than the first. There were only three ships in that one—a large vessel known as a carrack, and two smaller boats that the sailors called caravels. Now, a year later, a total of 17 proud ships crashed along with the westerly wind. Rolling this way and that, the boats heaved through the waves. The men in the fleet could look out over the sea and count three carracks and 14 caravels. It was the largest body of ships yet sent across the Atlantic Ocean. No one had ever tried such a large undertaking. A few craft now and again had pressed westward in the past. Sometimes they were fishing boats. Sometimes they were ships blown off course. Just a year before, the expedition was a small one to trace out a new trade route to Asia. Nothing to date had been all that special. The ships this day, however, were an awesome sight. And still, for all their majesty and grace, out in the middle of the vast blue-green sea the ships bobbed along like so many wooden corks. They floated along on water that, as one observer noted, gleamed brighter than "polished marble."[1]

A brilliant azure sky hung overhead, decorated here and there with gentle white puffs of clouds. But darker clouds along the horizon indicated that land was not far off. One of the men on the ships recalled observing "a considerable change in the sky and the wind, with dark, threatening clouds ahead." Such signs convinced the fleet's commander that "they were close to land,"[2] as did the stiff breeze that carried cackling seagulls over the ships. Seabirds on

An expedition of Christopher Columbus's leaves the port of Palos in Spain. A young Juan Ponce de León took part in Columbus's second voyage to the New World in 1493.

the wing were another good omen. The sailors knew that birds grew more plentiful as land got closer. So, they watched with relief as one gull after another twisted and spun along behind the ships. Occasionally they came careering over the decks. The birds seemed like angels, in a way. It was almost as if they had come to the rescue of the men. The sailors had been out to sea far longer than they had wanted. Every beat of the gray and white wings echoed like applause, like a happy greeting. Nature seemed to be clapping for the sailors, welcoming them back to dry land. Each man on the decks celebrated quietly in his heart. He had made it. The ships had made it. The fleet was there. The weary seafarers lifted their eyes and imagined land just over the horizon.

The sea wind on which the birds flew was a riot of different scents. Blended together into a luscious mix, all the aromas of the tropics blew in over the tossing ships. One moment, the sailors could just barely detect a hint of sea salt in the air. The next, a whiff of tropical flowers drifted under their noses. Blossoms and fruits could almost be picked whole out of the air. Their fragrances put such treasures almost within reach. Land, everyone thought, certainly could not be far off now. The sweet smells promised rest, comfort, and relaxation. Finally the tired men would escape the dank confines of their small, cramped vessels.

After weeks of fighting their way across the ocean, the exhausted seafarers joyfully anticipated the beauty of a Caribbean island. Of course there would be many dangers. The terrain was unknown to them. Wild animals and bizarre insects, some of them poisonous, lurked in the jungles. People, too, inhabited all of these islands, and not all of these natives welcomed visitors. In fact, many of them would rather kill the intruders from the sea than extend a hand in peace. The sailors had armed themselves for a reason.

And yet, the fresh breezes relentlessly pulled the ships in. Like immense emerald magnets, the islands grabbed the fleet and drew it toward the golden beaches that just now were coming into view. The men could have stood there all day, enjoying the invigorating aromas and reveling in the lovely sights. But urgent tasks screamed out for their attention. The needs of the ships drove them back to work like some merciless master.

Each of the 17 ships that day was a beehive of activity. Sailing vessels in the late fifteenth century required a lot of attention. Not a moment passed that was not filled with one job or another. Seamen scampered over the decks. They climbed like monkeys over the rigging and through the forest of masts. Busy deckhands pulled on ropes, set sails, and worked the boats as if they were lumbering musical instruments. Sweating in the sun, the men raced about doing all the tasks that sailors did to keep their ship on course. The few officers, directing all this hustle and bustle, stood on decks and ladders barking orders. With stern looks, they demanded quick replies to each command. The pace of the work and the excitement grew as the thin coastline rose slowly above the western horizon. Soon they would be there. Land! Land, ho! Due West!

Near the wheel of the flagship stood the commander of this flotilla. He was as happy as his men that their voyage was almost over. Far-flung journeys thrilled the captain, but they were tiring. His family had a history of traveling here and there, and the man standing proudly on deck this day was no different. He loved the adventure and excitement of exploration. He longed to see new people and places, to find new answers to old questions. Now his hardy ships were finally approaching the very islands that he himself discovered just a year before. No, this was not his first trip westward from Europe. He had done all this before. In 1492, he led the expedition that won these islands in an uncharted sea for the king and queen of what would someday be Spain. For that historic mission of discovery, the leader was granted the title Admiral of the Ocean Sea. His name was Don Cristóbal Colón—Christopher Columbus.

Many historians have studied Columbus. Yet to catch a glimpse of the subject of this biography you would have to look past Columbus. You would need to peek over his shoulder as he stood there on the ship's bridge. Our man was there, in a crowd of unwanted passengers whom Columbus ignored. They were aboard the ships that day through no choice of the admiral's. The government official who had organized the expedition sold spots on the journey as a way to enrich himself. He never asked Columbus if he wanted the extra men along. But here they were, dozens of young adventurers seeking fame and fortune in the New World.

Columbus was stuck with them. They did not distract him too much, though. The admiral paid no attention to them as he looked toward the horizon. He was too busy watching the islands in front of him grow larger with each passing league. So were they. The passengers' anticipation rose as they strained to see the place that awaited them. The ships' decks became virtual viewing platforms. The rails were a jumble of craning necks and bumping shoulders. It was here that a special young man jostled for a place. He was excited and eager to step out on the distant shore. He labored to catch a glimpse of the tropical stage on which he would act out his life's drama.

The young man up on deck that day should not have even been there. His place among the ship's company was gained through some pretty sharp dealing. Columbus's first voyage to the New World had been well planned. His crews had been carefully selected. This second time around, however, preparations had been left to a corrupt politician named Juan Rodriguez de Fonseca. He was a bishop of the Catholic Church, but he was not a very holy man. Fonseca was, according to someone who knew him, "very capable in the management of the things of this world."[3] That meant that he wanted money. Fonseca loved luxury and hated Columbus. He envied the admiral's success and wanted some of Columbus's fame for himself. Fonseca also desired part of the fortune that might come from finding a sea route to Asia. Quietly, the bishop set out to ruin Columbus and make himself rich in the process.

Fonseca tried his best to wreck the second voyage to America. He stole supplies destined for Columbus's fleet and replaced them with shoddy substitutes. The wily bishop took money from the expedition's accounts and used it to buy himself nice clothes. Perhaps worst of all, Fonseca took bribes from hundreds of greedy men who wanted to tag along with Columbus. Most of these "gentlemen adventurers" were only out to get some of the riches they believed were waiting across the ocean. But at least one of them had other plans. He was not that interested in wealth for its own sake. He craved danger and excitement as much as gold. So, here he was, on the deck of one of Columbus's ships waiting to go ashore.

From his beginnings as a "gentleman adventurer" on Columbus's expedition, Ponce de León went on to found Puerto Rico and discover Florida.

This young, ambitious Castilian dreamed of a life as a conqueror. He imagined sailing the western seas. He saw himself subduing ferocious savages. He anticipated getting lots of fancy titles, influence, and power. Fresh from the wars against the Muslims back home, he was hungry for new challenges. No one knew who he was. Standing on the ship's deck that morning in 1493, this "gentleman" had no idea what the future held. He certainly did not know that he would become one of the most famous explorers in history. He never imagined that his deeds would be remembered for centuries. Cities and towns would someday bear his name. Schoolchildren would learn about his exploits and write reports on his life. He would be famous.

Long after Columbus's last trip to the New World, this eager young man went to work. He built a family and a fortune on a newly settled island. He used his sharp wits to become important in government. He explored a large chunk of the Caribbean Sea. He rose to the rank of governor and served his country faithfully. He fought, bled, and eventually died for Spain. Puerto Rico credits this incredible man as its founder. Most famously, he became the discoverer of Florida. He sailed into history as he sailed the seas. His friends knew him as Juan—the man we know today as Juan Ponce de León.

Test Your Knowledge

1   What is a caravel?
    a. A navigational tool
    b. A type of gun
    c. A sailing ship
    d. None of the above

2   What did the appearance of gulls mean to
    Columbus's crew?
    a. They were running short on supplies.
    b. Land was near.
    c. The expedition was doomed.
    d. None of the above.

3   Who was Juan Rodriguez de Fonseca?
    a. A friend and sponsor of Christopher Columbus
    b. A corrupt politician and bishop
    c. A gentleman adventurer who sailed with
        Columbus
    d. None of the above

4   How did Ponce de León come to join the Columbus
    expedition?
    a. He was a stowaway.
    b. He was a close friend of Columbus's.
    c. He bought a place on the expedition
        from Fonseca.
    d. None of the above.

5   Why did Fonseca try to ruin Columbus's
    second journey to the New World?
    a. He disliked Columbus, and wanted to
       make money by short-changing Columbus
       on supplies.
    b. He wanted to go instead of Columbus.
    c. He was ordered by King Ferdinand to
       sabotage the journey.
    d. None of the above.

ANSWERS: 1. c; 2. b; 3. b; 4. c; 5. a

A New Spain and a New World

Juan Ponce de León is usually called a "Spanish" explorer. This makes sense today. Spain is what we call the place where Ponce de León was born. But in his day, things were different. Back then, there was no single place known as Spain. Instead, the area that would become Spain was really two lands. Spain, in effect, was broken into two parts. Not until 1516 did a unified kingdom that was named Spain exist. It is more accurate, then, to say that Ponce de León's Spain was part of the Iberian Peninsula. Or, better yet, it was the kingdoms of Castile and Aragon.

Iberia is the part of Europe that stretches from the Pyrenees Mountains in the north to the Strait of Gibraltar in the south. For most of Ponce de León's life, this sunny, pleasant peninsula was split into three kingdoms. Castile and Aragon shared their home with the kingdom of Portugal. Portugal, of course, went its own way. Castile and Aragon became Spain. They eventually joined together, but that was all in the future. For the time being, Castile and Aragon were very different. Each had its own kings and queens. Each had its own government and laws. The people who lived in the kingdoms had little in common. Their cultures, or ways of life, were not the same. In some areas, even the languages were a bit different.

Spain, in the late fifteenth century, existed only in its parts. And those parts argued with one another all of the time. They fought over land rights and trade, and often just out of simple pride. Only one thing pulled everyone together—the Muslims. Very few Spaniards liked the Moors, the Muslims who had invaded Iberia in the eighth century. They brought strange ways to the peninsula. The Muslims were distrusted as foreigners and hated as non-Christians. They did not believe, like the Iberian Christians, that Jesus was the Son of God. The Muslims followed the religion of Islam. Their god was Allah. The Muslims worshipped Allah and promised to defend their faith. Christians feared Islam and resented the presence of its followers. Castilians and Aragonese alike, therefore, had a burning desire to expel the Muslims. They should go back where they came from, most Christians felt. Muslims occupied all of North Africa, and Islam seemed almost natural there. But Spain was another matter entirely. The native religion of Spain was Christianity. The Christians felt that the land belonged to them. So having Muslims on Christian soil was an insult. It posed a direct challenge, they argued, to the European way of doing things.

The church and the Christian kings feared the Muslims as much as everybody else. Even though Islam was a religion, religion and politics went together in the fifteenth century. The church and the state everywhere shared power. So, threaten one and you threatened the other. Kings and popes, in short, came as a set in the late Middle Ages. They helped each other get what they needed. Europe's kings, to begin with, depended upon the church for support. Whenever the people would ask why the king was king, the church said that God wanted it that way. If you disobeyed the king or queen, then that was just like disobeying God. In return, the kings and queens ordered their subjects to do what the church said and obey the pope. When a person challenged the power of the church, they really rebelled against the king. Church and state could not be separated. The king and the pope, in the end, occupied the same place in the social order.

THE MUSLIM CHALLENGE

Internal threats to the power of church and state were dealt with quickly and often violently. So were external ones, especially those that spelled trouble for the religious and political leaders. That is just what Islam did. With Muslim armies in the region, no one was safe. Islam, put another way, could not be viewed as just a political or religious danger. It was both. If the most important parts of society were under attack, a defense would have to be mounted. A Muslim presence in Spain could not be tolerated. The warriors of Islam, Spain's Christians agreed, would have to go.

The Christians did not wait long. They started trying to get rid of the Muslims soon after Islam arrived in the year 711. Oddly enough, the Muslims were originally asked to come. A group of Iberian nobles had invited the Muslims in from North Africa. They had been fighting over land and power. It was hoped that the Muslims might settle matters once and for all. They did. A Muslim army crossed the Strait of Gibraltar and quickly gobbled up most of what would someday be Spain. Centuries passed, and the Muslims did not budge. They liked it just fine where they were.

The Iberian Muslims did not have much contact with others of their faith. They were far from the center of Islam in the Middle East. They also had little contact with the local Christians. This meant that the Iberian Muslims slowly developed their own lifestyle. Islamic Spain, on its own, "produced great monuments, learned men and philosophers."[4] In every way, the Muslims made their own ways of living and praying to their God. The beauty of their cities and mosques was unsurpassed. Schools and libraries flourished. Islamic Spain became a center of learning and art. The rest of Europe did not have much of either. The Muslim armies also became more powerful. All this added to the popular hatred of the Muslims. Eventually the Christians could not take it anymore. They decided to strike back. From their castles near the border with France, they marched out to reclaim what had once been theirs.

War broke out between the Christians and Muslims for control of the land they shared. The Christians fought hard and over time gained the advantage. As the years passed, the Christian forces pressed relentlessly southward. The Muslims, who could not call for reinforcements from other Muslim countries, had no choice but to fall back. In time, they stopped retreating and settled down to defend an area that surrounded the city of Granada. It did not matter, though. Year after year the war dragged on, and slowly the area that the Muslims controlled

Spanish forces conquer the Moors at Pamplona. The expulsion of the Moors from the Iberian Peninsula gave money, land, and people to King Ferdinand and Queen Isabella. And the kingdom became ready to explore the western sea.

grew smaller and smaller. By the middle of the fifteenth century, things were bad for the Muslims. It became clear to everyone that sooner or later they would lose. "Islamic Spain," as one writer has concluded, "fell into disunion and the reconquest of the peninsula began." [5] Spain, when it actually came into being, would belong only to the Christians.

COMPETITION EVERYWHERE

The Muslim war, however, was only part of the story. Another less violent conflict helped set the stage for Ponce de León's adventures. Castile and Aragon had kept one eye on Portugal while they fought the armies of Islam. Their western neighbor had become a problem. But it was not really Portugal's fault. Current events put it into the place it was in. The Muslims, by the fifteenth century, controlled the Middle East. That made it hard for Europeans to get goods from China, and Portugal benefited from this. Italy had once been the gateway to Asia. Now, it was to be Portugal's turn. The old trade routes through Italy stopped working, and that caused European merchants "to turn their eyes in other directions." [6] They looked toward Portugal.

The Muslims made it harder to trade with China over the ancient Silk Road. Yet trade had to go on. If land routes did not work anymore, then it would have to be by water. The Atlantic Ocean, it followed, naturally got more attention. Someone, some European kingdom, people argued, was going to have to try to sail to Asia. Only then could Muslim territory be avoided. Someone would have to go literally around the other side of the earth. Such an effort would be not be safe or easy, but it might bring in great wealth. The first kingdom to open a sea route to China, in fact, might just control all of the trade with the East. That meant money. Whoever found a new, secure way to China could get very rich.

A prize like this caught everyone's eye. People along the Atlantic coast started making plans, plans that had one goal—to grab the wealth of Asia before someone else did. And no kingdom moved faster than Portugal. It jumped on the chance to make money off new trade routes. Portugal wanted to turn the Atlantic and Indian Oceans into highways heading east, *Portuguese* highways. Beginning in 1415, Portugal sent waves of explorers and traders out to sea. These men claimed land and earned cash for the Portuguese king.

It was only natural that Portugal's next-door neighbors looked to get in on the action. Castile and Aragon did not want Portugal to get all of the benefits of Atlantic trade; they wanted some, too. The problem was the Muslims. While they were in Iberia, Castile and Aragon were stuck. Before the two kingdoms could get rich, they would have to get rid of the intruders. They had been working toward that goal for a while, and now was time to pick up the pace. Castile and Aragon needed to chase out the Muslims for good. They could then put some of their own explorers out into the Atlantic.

The beginning of the end for Spain's Muslims came in 1469. Ferdinand, the prince of Aragon, married Isabella, the princess of Castile. Their union brought the forces of Christian Spain together. A single push could now be made against the enemy. A unified monarchy, it was felt, could easily throw out the Muslims. Then Ferdinand and Isabella would rule a new Spain. A new people would emerge. They would be men and women who could proudly call themselves Spanish. As

Ferdinand put it after the wedding, "Now . . . we are all brothers." [7]

The future looked good, but there was still much to do. Isabella's brother, the king of Castile, did not approve of her marriage. He did not like the idea of joining up with Aragon, because the Aragonese had been enemies in the past. Now they would be countrymen. This was a sour thought for the king.

A Royal Wedding

In the middle of October 1469, two young lovers met in the Spanish city of Valladolid. No one noticed their arrival, and the couple tried hard to keep it that way. Neither the boy nor the girl wanted anyone to know they were there. They just happened to be a 17-year-old prince and an 18-year-old princess who came together that day for a very special event. They were going to be secretly married.

The wedding had to be in secret, since neither of the couple's families approved of it. In fact, the bride's brother had tried to lock her in her house, when he found out what she wanted to do. She virtually had to be kidnapped in order to be in Valladolid on the big day. Everything had to be

Still, even he knew that the two kingdoms would have to unite sooner or later. It was the only logical thing to do. National union would help both countries. When he finally died in 1474, the way was cleared for his kingdom and Aragon to come together. Ferdinand and Isabella could officially unite their crowns, and they would. That same year, oddly enough, little Ponce de León was possibly

done without anybody knowing. The few guests who were invited swore not to tell. They went so far as to come to the wedding in disguise.

Secrecy was only the start. Despite being royal children, the prince and princess were broke. They had almost no money of their own. All of their wealth belonged to their families, and they could not get to it. Each one of the newly-weds would be rich, but only after becoming king and queen. This did not matter either, though. Without money or permission, the boy and girl were still determined to be married. They stood ready to join hands and, before too long, the crowns of their two lands. Their names were Ferdinand and Isabella.

born (though several historians believe he may have been born as early as 1460).

Unfortunately, a niece of Isabella's named Juana immediately challenged Isabella's right to become queen. Juana was married to the Portuguese king, and she and her husband said that the throne belonged to her. She talked her husband into trying to take it when it became clear that Isabella would not give it up willingly. Portugal invaded Castile, and a five-year war broke out. This was double trouble. While battling her niece, Isabella and Ferdinand still had to go against the Muslims. Their armies had to fight against two enemies at the same time. They soon pushed back the Portuguese. At the same time they captured one Muslim stronghold after another. The Portuguese soldiers, after a while, went back to their kingdom. The Muslims found themselves bottled up. The Muslims held a mere handful of cities. Ferdinand and Isabella were on the edge of victory.

VICTORY AND COLUMBUS

Peace with Portugal came in 1479. Isabella's rule was confirmed. No sooner had Isabella become safe on her throne than Ferdinand accepted the crown of Aragon. Now, as king and queen, they ruled over a single place. Now they could deal with the Muslims. They prepared their armies for one last push. This time, Ferdinand and Isabella had total conquest on their minds. That thought carried them along for the next 13 years. These were long years of bitter war. In 1492, they won. Spain celebrated as the last Muslim city fell.

The reconquest of the Iberian Peninsula gave money, land, and people to Ferdinand and Isabella. Almost in an instant, the unified kingdom was ready to explore the vast western sea. With Spanish sailors out on the ocean, Portugal's monopoly on Atlantic exploration and trade would be shattered. Centuries of weakness and division were coming to an end. Profit and pride were ready for the taking. Ships stood in harbors like Cádiz and Seville, all set to sail westward. A national spirit of conquest, fed by the victory over Islam, began to grow. The rest of the world would soon see the Spanish flag flying over the waves. But the right sort of adventurers still needed to be found. Hardy and fearless explorers were needed.

Spain needed men like the Italian Columbus, and the local boy, Juan Ponce de León.

Columbus had talked to Ferdinand and Isabella in the 1480s about sailing west in an effort to reach Asia. They refused to help him because they were still at war with the Muslims. Now, the monarchs were eager to finance any voyage that might undercut the Portuguese. They eventually said yes when Columbus asked a second time. They even gave him the money and ships to make his attempt. In fact, the king and queen ordered Columbus to go out and explore "certain parts of the Ocean Sea."[8] Whatever land he found, he was free to govern as he wished. If he found gold, however, Columbus had to give most of it to the king and queen. Of all the "pearls, precious stones, gold, silver, [and] spices" he might uncover, Columbus could only keep 10 percent.[9] Ferdinand and Isabella had made a very good deal.

Columbus sailed that same year. After several weeks at sea, he made landfall in October 1492. Columbus landed at either San Salvador or another island close by named Samana Cay. No one is really sure which it was. The admiral himself believed that he had reached the East Indies. He continued to believe this till the day he died. His error, though, did not stop him from sailing all over the Caribbean Sea. Columbus eventually made four voyages to the New World. Each brought Spain closer to empire. Every time Columbus returned home he brought news of strange lands and people—and tales of gold. When he reported to the king and queen, he showed them "crowns of gold, large masks decorated with gold, ornaments of beaten gold, nuggets of gold, [and] gold dust." [10] Nothing attracted fifteenth- and sixteenth-century Europeans like gold. To get it they would do just about anything. Gold became the center of Spanish attention and activity in the New World.

Ferdinand and Isabella moved quickly to get their share of that gold. They just as quickly claimed the ground it lay in. In 1494, the pope actually split the Western Hemisphere into two halves. One part went to Portugal, the other to Spain. The goal for both kingdoms was a secure source of wealth. Yet for Ferdinand and Isabella there was more. They hoped to enrich Spain only as a means to greater ends. The king and queen

King Ferdinand of Aragon and Queen Isabella of Castile married in secret as teenagers. Their marriage united the two most powerful regions in what would become Spain.

imagined that someday Spain might dominate all of Europe. This did not, of course, mean that Spain would actually conquer the other European kingdoms. Rather, Ferdinand and Isabella saw a future where what Spain wanted came first. They hoped to do this by making the Spanish economy the strongest in all of Europe. Prosperity would allow Spain to dominate its neighbors.

A united, wealthy Spain would lead the Western world. All that was needed to pull this off was gold and lucrative trade routes to Asia. Spain could get gold right away, but it would eventually run out. Trade with the East, on the other hand, would bring in large sums of money for decades. Spain would get rich! Unfortunately, there was stiff competition in this arena. Just about every other kingdom with access to the ocean wanted to control the Asian market as well. Portugal had its eyes on the Atlantic. Soon France, England, and the Netherlands would, too. Spain could join in, but developing its own trade networks would take time. In the meanwhile, Spain needed cash. That is where the gold came in.

Getting as much glittering gold as possible became a top priority. It drove Ferdinand and Isabella to look more closely at the New World. Columbus was only the start. He opened the New World, but others would pull the wealth from it. Columbus's real contribution, in fact, was in setting up a Spanish base of operations. He founded the first Spanish colony on the island of Hispaniola. From there, explorers could fan out in search of gold, the gold that Columbus reported as being everywhere in the Americas. He made it seem as if all you had to do was reach down and grab it. The men who followed Columbus, then, dreamed of finding gold quickly and easily. Trade routes were important, but only the promise of immediate wealth would make them possible.

The kings who came after Ferdinand and Isabella sent more Spanish explorers across the sea. Every year, so it seemed, ships left Spain carrying men with visions of heaps of gold in their heads. As each new fleet sailed away, gold became more important to the Spanish. Men like Vasco Núñez de Balboa and Hernán Cortés risked their lives trying to find places that might prove full of it. They and other fortune-seekers concentrated on what is today Mexico and Central America, because local Indians pointed them in that direction. There, the Indians said, the Spanish would discover virtual kingdoms of gold. Other places were pretty much ignored, but Mexico did indeed prove to be very rich. The Aztec

Empire there was indeed weighed down by all of its gold. The Aztecs, who saw it as only a shiny rock, offered some to Cortés when he arrived. He, of course, wanted much more than a gift, and quickly captured all of it. But while vast piles of gold were being taken from the Aztecs, a young Ponce de León turned his eyes to the north. This was where his name would be made, the adventurer thought. While others went west, he would go north. Ponce de León would surely find his fortune and fame in the New World, but he would find them where no one else was looking.

Test Your Knowledge

1 In the fifteenth century, Spain was
   a. a unified democracy ruled by a parliament.
   b. a region of two kingdoms: Aragon and Castile.
   c. a unified kingdom under a single monarch.
   d. a group of feudal states governed by
      the church.

2 Why did the Muslims originally come to the
   region that is now Spain?
   a. They were invited by Iberian nobles.
   b. They invaded in hopes of spreading Islam.
   c. They invaded in search of gold and riches.
   d. None of the above.

3 After years of battle, the Christians forced the
   Muslims to retreat to a small area around
   what city?
   a. León
   b. Castile
   c. Granada
   d. Madrid

4 Why was finding a sea route to China and the
   Far East so important?
   a. Europe was broke and in need of supplies.
   b. Muslims in the Middle East made the overland
      trade routes dangerous.

c. The church wanted to gain new Christian converts in China.

d. None of the above.

5 Why did Ferdinand and Isabella sponsor Columbus's expeditions?

a. They wanted to spread the Catholic faith.

b. They wanted to establish colonies in the New World.

c. They wanted to boost Spain's wealth, status, and influence.

d. None of the above.

Answers: 1. b; 2. a; 3. c; 4. b; 5. c

A Young
Adventurer

Ponce de León's early life is something of a mystery. Little information about him was written down. In the fifteenth century, little was written about most people. Accurate records of birth and death were maintained, but beyond that the government recorded almost nothing about people's daily lives. People certainly did not write much about themselves. Literacy, and more specifically writing, was a skill that few average people possessed. Even many nobles found it difficult to put down on paper what they and their families had done. So, diaries, journals, and such were scarce. When someone died, not much information was left behind.

Very little, therefore, is known reliably about Ponce de León's childhood and his distant ancestors. It seems, though, that his father, Pedro, descended from minor nobility. His family line might have even gone all the way back to ancient Rome. In fact, Pedro was quite proud to carry the title Fourth Lord of Villagarcía. Ponce de León's mother similarly had some noble blood in her veins. Doña Leonor de Figueroa, as she was known when she married Pedro, was the daughter of the Lord of Salvaleon. He was an influential man, and his family was rich. Salvaleon's daughter, as a result, brought a lot of money with her into her marriage with Pedro. More important, she gave her new husband a connection to the powerful Guzman clan. This clan was also known as the House of Toral, and Leonor's family was part of it. Ponce de León appears to have had some important relatives, and that proved crucial to his success. At critical points in his life, Ponce de León turned to his mother's side of the family for help.

All of these high-sounding titles and useful connections, however, did not translate into a privileged life for Ponce de León. His family had money, but not so much that they could really relax. Today, they would be considered pretty much middle class. Put another way, Ponce de León's parents had a name, but little immediate wealth. This meant that they had almost no political power of their own. Money has always bought influence. Leaders tend to listen more closely to rich people. In the fifteenth century, however, riches translated into direct political control of society. Lacking in money and influence, few people paid much attention to Ponce de León's family. Later on, the Guzman tie would come in handy, but not right now. As a boy, it did him little good. Taken together, it would be accurate to say that Ponce de León grew up in relative obscurity.

GROWING AND LEARNING
IN FIFTEENTH-CENTURY SPAIN

The future explorer's boyhood training was pretty

standard. Today, Ponce de León would have gone to school. He would have learned lessons and studied subjects. But Ponce de León lived at a very different time. Like other boys in fifteenth-century Spain, young Ponce de León probably had almost no formal education. Maybe he read some philosophy and history with a tutor. He might have studied a little Greek and Latin. That would have been the extent of it. He certainly read the Bible and went to church. Religion was central to people's lives in early modern Europe. Even if Ponce de León did not always act like a good Christian, he would have respected and feared the church. He never would have dreamed of challenging its authority or teachings.

Ponce de León's cultural lessons did not come from a book either; he learned them firsthand. It is known that he had relatives in the city of Cádiz, and that he visited there on occasion. Such trips to visit his relatives in the port city gave Ponce de León some exposure to ways other than his own. Traveling through Spain also gave him a strong sense of loyalty to the crown and kingdom. Ponce de León, as a result, grew up to be a very patriotic young

This photograph shows the cathedral in the port city of Cádiz, Spain. Ponce de León had relatives in Cádiz whom he visited. The trips exposed the young explorer to ways and customs other than his own.

man. So even if he did not attend school, he knew about his world. There was more to education in Ponce de León's day than classroom instruction and book learning. Boys, with a bit of nobility in their past, looked beyond books to real life for their training.

This real-world training for little Juan would have begun in the presence of his father. Later it would extend to the larger community of adult men. Boys in Ponce de León's day commonly came to know life by watching their fathers and other men. They stood by and observed how grown men acted everyday in business and in politics. By doing this, boys learned how to behave, what to do, and what to expect as they moved into manhood. They learned in the most physical sense—by example. Boys asked questions and listened carefully to the answers.

They also listened to the stories men told. These often touched on the war with the Muslims. Such tales spoke of the exploits of brave men fighting for their God and king. They were exciting and filled with adventure. It is not surprising that just about every boy dreamed of someday doing his part for the defense of Spain. Thousands of would-be warriors waited their turn to fight the dreaded Moors. That meant a whole different type of education, one that prepared a boy for battle and conquest.

ALMOST A KNIGHT

"Ponce de León," one of his biographers wrote, "was a product of the feudal knighthood system." He was taught the art of war, and even as a little boy he wanted to fight for his homeland. Determined to be a conqueror one day, Ponce de León "was trained in warfare from an early age."[11] Such training was hard and took a long time.

The process of becoming a Christian warrior began the same way for all boys hoping to become

One Day a Knight

Pero Niño sat respectfully in front of the old man. He was filled with awe. This was his teacher, a wise tutor filled with knowledge. Pero was honored to be with him, but the boy was also curious. He wondered what advice his teacher had to give him. The old man always had such important things to say. The man took boys and made them into knights by giving them the courage to take risks and have confidence in themselves.

Today, he would speak about some very important subjects for a future knight like Pero. He would talk about God and duty. "My son," the teacher began, "take note of my words, instruct your heart in my sayings and retain them, for later you will understand them." As Pero gave him all of his attention, the teacher continued.

knights, with training in the ways of honor, duty, and virtue. One teacher, for example, taught his students to be fearless and brave. Potential knights, he told them, had to be both. Boys should "serve the king," he said. Duty was a priority. Above all, they must "fear not death. . . . Death is good for the good

"Above all, know God," he said, "then yourself, then others." Look to nature he told Pero, and find God there. Serve your king, and be obedient to the God who made everything possible. The teacher reminded his young student that God gave each man "command and power [over] all the things that He created in the sea and on land."*

Go out into the world God gave us, the tutor concluded, discover what is around you, and always do your best. Knowledge, God, duty— that made a boy into a man, and a man into a great man. Pero learned this lesson well, as would Ponce de León.

* Kenneth R. Scholberg, *Spanish Life in the Late Middle Ages* (Chapel Hill: University of North Carolina Press, 1965), 79.

man because he goes to receive the reward for his goodness."[12] Another instructor told his boys to look to the "example from the knight St. James." This man urged his students to serve God as well as Spain. He wrote that they "must be ready to suffer all the tortures that may befall you" in the course of fighting Islam.[13] When the big push against the Muslims came, Spanish boys like Juan Ponce de León would be ready.

The campaign waged by Ferdinand and Isabella was hard-fought. It also drew many young nobles to the royal cause. Among those men was Pedro Nuñez de Guzman, one of Ponce de León's relatives. A member of the House of Toral, Nuñez de Guzman had a good reputation, but not a lot of money. Like many of his friends, he had land and a name, but no ready cash. One writer noted that Nuñez de Guzman barely had any income "despite the fact that he was of illustrious blood."[14] Still, he scraped together enough money to arm himself for battle. He probably even went into debt, but the privilege of fighting for Christian Spain was worth it.

He also hired a squire, a kind of fighting servant. Squires helped warriors with camp chores. They also tended to the soldiers' needs in battle, holding horses, sharpening swords, and the like. Sometimes, if a battle were going poorly, squires might even enter the fray, and do some fighting themselves. No matter what they did, squires constituted an important part of fifteenth-century European armies. These invaluable helpers were almost always ambitious boys. Fresh from their informal civilian education, and some training in knightly ways, squires signed on with a warrior to learn how to fight. This was the case with Nuñez de Guzman's boy. His squire was certainly ambitious, and eager to learn. He was 14-year-old Ponce de León.

Ponce de León stayed in Nuñez de Guzman's service for five years. During that time he lived through a good deal of combat. No official records of his service exist. It appears, however, that he saw serious action during the campaign to retake the city of Granada. He was almost certainly present during the actual capture of the city in 1492. Like every Christian in Spain, he was happy to see the Muslims go. People had looked forward to their expulsion for hundreds of years. It was a great day for Spain, but the defeat of Islam also meant that Ponce de León became unemployed. A few months later, while the celebrations continued, Columbus set sail from Palos on his famous voyage of discovery. Ponce de León missed that trip. He was busy trying to get a new job. Yet everything he tried bored him. He soon "longed for something more exciting." [15] He found it in 1493, on Columbus's second visit to the New World.

Columbus's initial trip was such a great success that he quickly won royal approval for another. Ferdinand and Isabella were very pleased with the job he did. They were especially happy with all the talk of gold. Their plans for Spain depended upon a steady flow of cash. If Columbus's stories were true, America would be the source of that money. The king and queen were more than happy to give Columbus a new fleet, and send him on his way. When he left, Columbus carried with him the hopes of his monarchs and countrymen. He took Juan Ponce de León along, too.

TO THE NEW WORLD

Columbus's second voyage was nothing like his first. This trip was a disorganized, chaotic affair. Nothing seemed to work out as planned. The problems started, of course, with Fonseca's misconduct. Indeed, most of the things that went wrong could be traced back to this one corrupt official. Columbus's mismanagement, however, doubtless made the expedition harder than it needed to be. He might have been a great explorer, but Columbus was a horrible administrator. The journey was so troubled that most of its "gentlemen adventurers," including Ponce de León, sailed home as soon as they could. Few men wanted anything more to do with a project that was rapidly turning into a real mess.

Columbus's second voyage was only a marginal success. The admiral's third trip to the New World was even worse. At one point, a group of colonists rose up against Columbus himself, and sent him back to Spain in chains. But the uproar eventually settled down after the king and queen personally stepped in. They ordered a reorganization of their Caribbean colonies, in particular the island of Hispaniola.

It was to a restructured Hispaniola, then, that Ponce de León returned in 1502. No one knows why he went back, or what he had been doing for the previous nine years. He probably missed the adventure and moneymaking opportunities of the

New World. Life in Spain for an unemployed soldier was dull, and also not very rewarding. Ponce de León would never get rich at home, so going back to the Americas probably looked good to him. Whatever the reason, Ponce de León arrived in the islands at a difficult moment. A rebellion among the Indians of Hispaniola had broken out soon after Columbus visited the island in June. Although some Taino Indians had made friends with the Spanish, others had not. Most Tainos, in fact, worried that the Spanish would be trouble. These people "saw the handwriting on the wall," one historian has said, "and launched armed uprisings against" the Spanish.[16]

The colony's governor, Nicolás de Ovando, moved quickly to crush the rebellion. He gathered together a small army and put it under the command of a soldier named Juan de Esquivel. Esquivel's mission was to smash the rebels. No Spaniard could tolerate a challenge to the power of the Spanish crown and the church. Esquivel promised the governor that the Indian rebellion would be extinguished. He gathered his forces and moved out. One of his lieutenants was an eager Ponce de León. Ponce de León had nothing against the Indians as

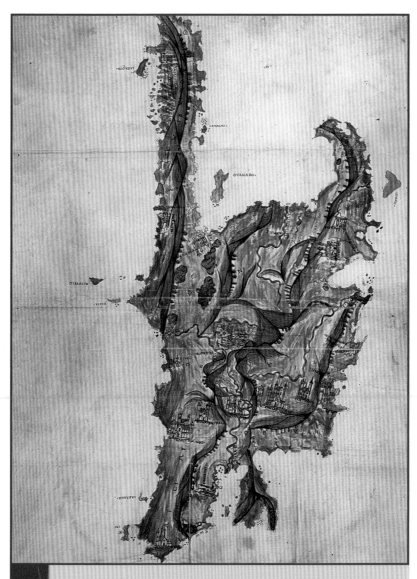

A Spanish map from Columbus's time shows the island of San Domingo, where he landed. In 1502, Ponce de León returned to Hispaniola. There, he helped quell an Indian rebellion and was rewarded for his service.

people; he did not particularly like the idea of attacking those he considered to be inferior fighters. The Muslims were one thing, a bunch of disorganized "savages" was another. Ponce de León would get no personal satisfaction from their destruction. He only wanted to impress Esquivel and the governor. Perhaps, Ponce de León hoped, good service would lead to rewards. Faithful, brave soldiers often received money and land after a successful campaign. Material gain, in money and influence, gave Ponce de León a reason to take up his sword.

The fighting that followed was more like a slaughter than combat between equals. The native Tainos were horribly outmatched. They were armed with primitive weapons. They lacked armor, horses, and organization. The Spanish, therefore, had little trouble defeating them. Indian arrows did nothing against the steel armor and guns of the Spanish soldiers. There never was a real battle to speak of, just Spanish troops shooting down Indians. But when it was all over, Esquivel and his men claimed a glorious victory. None cheered as loudly as Ponce de León. He had served well and waited for the prizes to be handed out. They were, and Ponce de

León got more than he expected. As a recent writer has noted, the Indian rebellion "catapulted Juan Ponce toward his place in history." [17]

Ponce de León got everything he desired. The crown awarded him a generous land grant for his service. Called an *encomienda*, it came with 225 acres of land and enough Indians to work it. The grant instantly transformed Ponce de León into a respected landowner. Just like that, the former squire could claim membership in the local elite. The gift also made him rich. Money and property gave Ponce de León power he never would have had otherwise. A new life began for him.

Test Your Knowledge

1 Ponce de León's early education probably included which of the following?
a. Instruction in Latin and Greek
b. Study of the Bible
c. Tutoring in philosophy and history
d. All of the above

2 How long did young Ponce de León serve as squire to Nuñez de Guzman?
a. Six months
b. One year
c. Five years
d. None of the above

3 Which of the following was part of a squire's job?
a. Helping his master with camp chores
b. Sharpening swords
c. Holding horses
d. All of the above

4 Which of the following best describes the battle between the Spanish and the Tainos?
a. The Tainos were well-organized and well-equipped warriors.
b. The primitive weapons of the disorganized Tainos were no match for the well-armed Spanish.

   c. Many of the Spanish soldiers deserted in
      combat.

   d. None of the above.

5 What did Ponce de León receive for his military
service to Juan de Esquivel?

   a. A land grant

   b. Gold doubloons

   c. A new noble title

   d. His own fleet of ships

ANSWERS: 1. d; 2. c; 3. d; 4. b; 5. a

A New Life
in a New Land

The Taino rebellion made Ponce de León a true gentleman adventurer. His service had given him land, money, and, above all, a respected name. All was going well, and Ponce de León's good fortune continued. The land he received from the government was very fertile. The soil on some of the Caribbean islands could be tough to work. Even after completing the arduous task of clearing the land, crops often did not grow well. Sometimes, they failed altogether. Ponce de León got very lucky with the land he received. Crops flourished in the dark, rich soil. Manioc and sweet potatoes, staples of the Caribbean diet, grew in abundance. The green pastures surrounding the farm fed a large herd of cattle. Cattle translated into beef and leather, two items the colonists had to have. It took almost no time for the sale of produce and livestock to give Ponce de León a small fortune. In fact, he made enough money to build a larger house on his property, thus turning it into an estate he named Salvaleón. The only thing missing in this pretty picture was a wife. But Ponce de León soon remedied that. He married a local girl named Leonor and began a family. Leonor eventually bore Ponce de León four children.

With children and an estate, Ponce de León settled down into a comfortable life by 1506. He counted himself among the elite landowners who controlled much of Spanish colonial society. He had plenty of leisure time, and all the money he needed. It would have been easy for him at this point to lean back and just enjoy life. That did not happen. Ponce de León was too much of a wanderer. He had, as the great writer Washington Irving once put it, an "impatience for quiet life."[18] Although he was well fed and rich, Ponce de León was bored. He yearned to get out and do something exciting again. The lure of adventure proved too much for him. Ponce de León could not remain still for long.

GOLD! GOLD! GOLD!

Reports of gold on nearby islands did not help. They stimulated Ponce de León's interest even more. He had heard all the thrilling rumors. Rare was the day when someone did not whisper something about a discovery of gold on this island or that. Stories of gold, just waiting to be scooped up, floated all over the place. Sailors and merchants claimed routinely that local Indians knew of vast piles of gold sitting just to the north and east of Hispaniola. Whoever set out after them would soon be a very rich man. The mysterious lands of the distant north were said to harbor huge stores of the precious yellow metal, but they were far away. Much closer was the little island of San Juan Bautista, just to the east of Hispaniola. Here, so the Indians said, gold lay about in vast quantities.

San Juan Bautista was only a short distance from Ponce de León's estate of Salvaleón on the coast of Hispaniola. Even an incompetent sailor would have had no difficulty navigating the stretch of water between Ponce de León's home and the reported hoards of gold. Certainly someone with Ponce de León's experience would be able to make the trip without a problem. He knew this himself. If he wanted to, Ponce de León thought, he could easily slip across the water and grab as much gold as he desired. An excited Ponce de León began pestering everyone around him for information about San Juan Bautista. He quizzed local Indians the hardest. Ponce de León was single-minded in his questioning.

The young adventurer's interest in what was known about San Juan Bautista, the island today called Puerto Rico, kept growing. He asked everyone about it, and his questions never failed to mention gold. When Ponce de León talked to his native workers, in particular, he demanded to know where the gold of San Juan was located, and who kept it. He "had information from that province and he wanted to know from the Indians who in the island . . . of San Juan had a lot of gold." [19] Yet as he badgered people about gold, something else stirred inside Ponce de León. He felt the urge to wander grow. He sensed fresh challenges, and craved new horizons to reach for. Life on the estate bored him. An expedition to an unexplored island was just what the restless young man needed.

Ponce de León decided to go. It did not matter that no one had given him permission to cross over to San Juan. He never asked for it, at least officially. Unofficially, the governor of Hispaniola told Ponce de León it was all right. They were friends, and the governor was happy to help out Ponce de León. So, with a wink from the royal authorities, he made out over the narrow strait that separated Hispaniola and San Juan. His expedition landed secretly on the coast, most likely in 1506, and immediately began searching for riches. He and his men found nothing, but scouted the island anyway. Hiking here and

(continued on page 62)

Bartolomé de Las Casas, a Spanish missionary and historian, was among the most vocal supporters of Indian rights among the Spanish. He implored his fellow settlers to be compassionate.

"Savages"

Were these people in the New World really human? Or were they brutes, fit only to be slaves? Questions like this swirled around Spain in the sixteenth century. No one had much of an idea what to do with the Indians. America was not supposed to be where it was; these new people were not supposed to exist. Yet here they were. Some in Spain said that the Indians were people just like them. In fact, these supporters, including the pope, said that the Indians were God's children, too, and should be treated as such. Others disagreed. They argued that the Indians were stupid savages. Their rightful place, according to those who did not like the Indians, was as slaves to the white Europeans.

Of all the Spaniards who supported Indian rights, Bartolomé de Las Casas spoke the loudest. Las Casas, a priest, begged his fellow Christians to be kind to the Indians. They were humans even if they looked and acted differently. Anyway, he wrote, people in Spain should remember that "we are just as barbarous to them as they to us."* Las Casas made a strong case for compassion.

Far more common, unfortunately, were the
arguments of those Spanish people who looked
at the Indians as almost being animals. "The
Indians," one such person wrote, "can be said to
be slaves of the Spaniards" and justly so. The
Spanish, he claimed, were "prudent and clever."
The Indians, on the other hand, were strong and
stupid; God made them that way. Indians were
best suited to "personal service"—slavery. **

These two views wrestled with each other.
The negative one eventually caught on. Even
though the Spanish accepted Indians as human,
they still made them slaves. No one ever asked
the Indians what they thought, but they let their
voices be heard. Indian uprisings against the
Spanish became common. The Native Americans
refused to be treated like animals. They fought
back. The Tainos were one group of resisters.
Their uprising worried the Spanish and made a
name for Ponce de León.

* J.H. Elliott, *The Old World and the New, 1492–1650*
(New York: Cambridge University Press, 1970), 48–49.
** Ibid., 44.

(continued from page 58)

there, the men gained valuable knowledge about the island's geography and inhabitants. Ponce de León felt satisfied as he returned home. He promised himself that he would come back later and find the gold he believed was there. A second trip, however, would have to be larger and more formal. He could not just sneak over to San Juan as he had the first time. He needed government approval on paper.

PAYING AN OFFICIAL VISIT

Ponce de León could not go on exploring in secret. He would never be able to lay claim to what he found if he found it without authorization. Ponce de León laid plans for a return to San Juan accordingly. In May 1508, he sent a petition directly to King Ferdinand in Spain asking for royal permission to go back to San Juan and hunt for gold. Somewhat to his surprise, the king readily agreed. The mission was approved. Now nothing could stop Ponce de León. He drew up some plans and wasted no time in getting underway.

Ponce de León gathered together crews and boats, and set sail in August 1508. This time, planning to stay a while, he also brought along some colonists to found a new settlement. He landed successfully on San Juan, and quickly set up a base of operations. No sooner had Ponce de León established his little outpost than he started barking orders left and right. He gave instructions and let everyone know just what he expected of them. Ponce de León, in essence, began acting as the island's governor. No one had appointed him to the position, but he was impatient. He wanted to put himself in charge before the governor on Hispaniola recalled him. That would effectively give the job to someone else. If gold were found, Ponce de León had to make sure that he had the first claim on it. As governor in his own right, he could do that. In addition, making himself governor might impress people back home. They might see him as more determined and serious about not only gold, but also a political career. Being a money-hungry, risk-taking adventurer was one thing; being a loyal servant of the crown was quite another. Ponce de León presented himself as the only realistic candidate for governor. Then, he waited for the king to appoint him.

That is exactly what happened. One year after his settlement of San Juan, the king confirmed Ponce de León as the island's royal governor. Ferdinand was impressed with Ponce de León's sense of purpose and his organizational skills. The king needed men like him in the New World. Ponce de León looked out for his own interests, but so did everyone else. At least Ponce de León was trustworthy. That was more than could be said of most other officeholders. The confirmation, however, was not made public. It was something of a secret between the king and Ponce de León. Christopher Columbus's son, Diego, who technically "owned" San Juan, certainly did not know of it. The islands in the vicinity of his father's discoveries were his by an early royal decree. Even if someone else landed on one, it remained Diego's. Ponce de León might have waded ashore, but Diego was determined to assert his claim. Diego Columbus, in short, did not care who explored San Juan; he demanded that his own man be in control. Ignoring Ponce de León altogether, Diego appointed a man named Juan Cerón as governor. As for Ponce de León, Diego Columbus ordered

An old Spanish painting shows Christopher Columbus with his two sons, Diego and Ferdinand. The islands in the vicinity of Columbus's discoveries were Diego's by royal decree. Diego Columbus and Ponce de León became embroiled in a dispute over control of Puerto Rico.

him to step aside, which he reluctantly did. Still, the explorer believed that he would win in the end. He had the king on his side. It took another year, but Ferdinand came to Ponce de León's assistance.

The king, in March 1510, sent a dispatch to the New World declaring Ponce de León to be San Juan's sole and rightful governor. In the end, any decision involving the Spanish colonies in the New World ended up with the king. Now he had spoken on the issue of San Juan. The king threw his support behind Ponce de León. In his letter of appointment, Ferdinand proclaimed Ponce de León the "Captain of sea and land and chief justice of the Island of San Juan."[20] Diego Columbus was furious, but what could he do? Ponce de León was obviously the king's favorite. Only one option was open to Diego–to go to court.

A TRULY ROYAL LAWSUIT

Although Spain was a monarchy, the king had to listen to the court of his royal council on legal matters. The court did not usually rule against the king. But if it did, he would give in. Aware of this, Columbus sued the king in 1511. If he could not win politically against Ponce de León, he would do so legally. Diego was desperate enough to take Ferdinand to court. The discoveries of his father were already fading into history by the second decade of the sixteenth century. Fewer and fewer people really cared who discovered the New World. As a result, Diego's influence and power were declining. If he did not move immediately, he might not have the influence to beat Ponce de León. Of course, many men in the king's government continued to like and respect Diego. They were sympathetic to his cause. His father's name carried some weight almost 20 years after his famous 1492 voyage. Ponce de León knew that as well as anyone did. The court battle would be tough.

The winner turned out to be Diego Columbus. The royal council settled the lawsuit on May 5, 1511, in Diego's favor. Columbus was now free to do as he wished on "his" island. He was given the authority, in fact, to do whatever he saw fit in all the territory left to him by his father. Diego could not wait to fire Ponce de León. He was looking forward to it. Yet when the news finally arrived on San Juan, Ponce de León took his removal in stride. Everyone was shocked. No one thought that the explorer would take the decision so well. The reason was that the king had spoiled Diego's surprise. Ferdinand had already written Ponce de León letting him know what Diego was up to. The king also let Ponce de León know which way the court was leaning. The now-former governor had prepared himself for the disappointment. Columbus was thrilled anyway. Ponce de León would remain San Juan's military commander, but that was it. His word no longer carried any royal authority. The island he had settled was taken away from him.

San Juan Bautista received its first flag and coat of arms in November 1511. The pro-Columbus governor, Juan Cerón, took office the same month. As Diego celebrated, Ponce de León sulked, and wondered what to do next. Ferdinand, his hands tied, urged the explorer to move on. Get on with other things, the king seemed to say. Ponce de León quickly took his advice. He remembered the rumors he had been hearing for a long time. Ponce de León recalled the tales of a large and mysterious island far to the north of Hispaniola. There might be great riches there, people had said, maybe gold. Ponce de León's spirit picked up. As a later biographer wrote, "what greater adventure could there be than seeking and conquering a new island."[21] His political career was on hold, so now would be a good time to check out other opportunities. If nothing else, a sea journey to distant shores would get him away from Columbus and all his schemes. Yes, the sea would be nice. Ponce de León began planning.

Test Your Knowledge

1 Which of the following best describes Ponce de León's estate?

    a. Infertile land that was difficult to farm

    b. A region of rocky waterfalls near which Ponce de León opened an inn

    c. Fertile farmland ideal for crops and cattle that made Ponce de León rich

    d. None of the above

2 What lured Ponce de León away from his family and comfortable estate?

    a. A commission to fight for Spain

    b. Rumors of gold waiting to be taken from nearby islands

    c. An extramarital affair

    d. The desire to find an all-water trade route to the Pacific

3 What is the current name for the island of San Juan Bautista?

    a. Haiti

    b. Cuba

    c. Puerto Rico

    d. St. Thomas

4 How did Ponce de León obtain official permission to explore San Juan Bautista?

   a. He bribed a local official.

   b. He forged the needed documents.

   c. He petitioned the king of Spain.

   d. None of the above.

5 Why did Diego Columbus sue the king of Spain?

   a. To challenge Ponce de León's authority over San Juan Bautista

   b. To obtain sole rights to explore the New World

   c. To get back pay owed to his father, Christopher Columbus

   d. None of the above

ANSWERS: 1. c; 2. b; 3. c; 4. c; 5. a

Finding Florida

Ponce de León was not the only man to wonder what lay north of San Juan. Many people had long been curious about the area. Some sailors might actually have gone there before Ponce de León. These early visitors were most likely slave traders searching for new victims or "merchandise" as the slavers called such unfortunate men and women. Bartolomé de Las Casas, a sixteenth-century priest who objected to the mistreatment of Indians, wrote that slave ships sailed north in 1511. "At the time," Las Casas claimed, slave traders came together "to go out and capture innocent people . . . [near] the land and coastline that we now call Florida."[22]

The evidence seems to indicate that others found Florida before Ponce de León, but only he would have official clearance to settle it. King Ferdinand had encouraged the explorer to leave San Juan, and he planned to. Ponce de León in 1511 petitioned the king for permission to go north, but he seemed to have caught Ferdinand off guard. For a full year, Ponce de León wrote letter after letter back to the royal court. Finally the king replied. Ferdinand issued an order for Ponce de León "to go to discover and settle the Islands" that were said to lie above Cuba.[23] He was also granted, without exception, "the government" of any newly discovered place "for all the days of your life."[24] There would be no repeat of the Diego Columbus episode. But there was more. Not only would Ponce de León be governor of the place he found, he could keep the wealth as well. Ferdinand assured the explorer that he could keep "the houses, farms, settlements, and property that you make there, and any gain derived. . . ."[25]

Ponce de León could not believe his good fortune. The king made him a governor, and potentially a very wealthy one at that. Yet the real prize was Ferdinand's guarantee that Diego Columbus's

A Northern Island

Ponce de León had to work with what he had. Every map that he opened showed the New World as a series of islands. Some were small; some were big. But they were all islands. Even those places that had not yet been explored were thought to be island chains. Columbus certainly thought so, as did his king, Ferdinand. Ferdinand believed that the entire western ocean was filled with islands of one type or another. That is why, when he wanted Ponce de León to sail northward, he gave the explorer "the authority to go and discover and settle the Islands of Biminy." He meant to say Bimini. Bimini is indeed an island, but it is a tiny one to the east of where Ponce de León intended to go.

hands would be tied. This island would be Ponce de León's. The king explicitly ordered that Ponce de León's old enemy was to "give [him] all the favor and aid that you may find necessary." Columbus, by the king's decree, had to swear that he would offer "no impediments to you in any shape or form." [26] Ponce de León did not have to worry about that pesky Diego Columbus anymore.

The Spanish called the whole north Bimini because they thought the first island was only one in a long chain that stretched across the Caribbean. These "islands" were believed to be densely populated and, best of all, loaded with gold. That is what drew everyone's attention, especially Ponce de León's. They imagined piles of gold spread out from one horizon to the other. They would be very disappointed in the end. There were no Islands of Biminy north of Cuba, sinking under the weight of all their gold and jewels. There was, however, a place called Florida.

PUTTING FLORIDA ON THE MAP

The explorer now focused all of his efforts on getting ready. He returned to Salvaleón in December 1512. Once there, he put his personal affairs in order. He gathered his ships and crews together next. The three ships he had—the *Santiago*, the *Santa Maria de la Consolación*, and the *San Cristóbal*—were fine and strong. The vessels carried 60 crew members drawn from every ethnic group imaginable. It was truly a diverse company of sailors. Indians, Africans, Europeans, and even one woman signed on with Ponce de León. He had plenty of hands on deck. Next came the supplies. Everything was ready by the spring of 1513. On March 4, the ships and their determined captain put to sea.

The warm waves heaved and rolled as the proud little fleet made its way north. Ponce de León's plan made allowances for frequent stops. Food and water would be taken on at small islands along the way. Ponce de León also brought plenty of paper. He hoped to map the entire route for future reference. It would slow him down, all that map-making, but Ponce de León did not care. The adventurer wanted a solid record of his trip. He himself and others might need a good map of the area in the years to come. Good maps took time to draw. Ponce de León wanted the job done properly. He was in no hurry. He could control his eagerness.

So, from March 4 to April 2, his ships skipped leisurely from island to island. They wound their way through narrow passages, floated over coral reefs, filled full sails across open water. At last, on April 3, the crew noticed that the water beneath them was getting shallower. The men very shortly sighted land. The ships slowed to a halt and dropped anchor off the coast of the place Ponce de León named La Florida. His landfall was somewhere on the eastern shore, south of modern-day Jacksonville. The adventurer chose the name because Florida "was very pretty to behold . . . [and] they discovered it in the time of the Feast of Flowers [Pascua Florida]."[27]

Five days after making his first landfall, Ponce de León went back to sea. He sailed north for a while, and then he turned around toward the south. Hugging the shoreline, his ships came upon an Indian village on April 20, 1513. Ponce de León decided to make contact. He planned to drop

Ponce de León relaxes on his 1513 expedition to Florida. He first made landfall south of modern-day Jacksonville. Ponce de León also encountered the Gulf Stream current during the voyage.

anchor and go ashore to meet the villagers. Yet at this point, a very strange thing happened. The ships "encountered a current that they were unable to sail against even though they had a strong wind." According to witnesses, "the current was so strong" that the ships' anchor chains almost broke.[28] Ponce de León, without even knowing it, had discovered the famous Gulf Stream that swirls through the North Atlantic.

Ponce de León's crews struggled to overcome the current, and eventually succeeded. They had gotten themselves out of some real trouble. More dangers, however, awaited them on land. The shore party that went to talk to the Indians received a hostile greeting. As the men waded onto the beach, a later account read, they were "called by the Indians who, in turn, tried to take the small boat, the oars, and arms." Ponce de León's men resisted. Next, a small fight broke out in which "the Indians hit a sailor on the head with a stick, knocking him unconscious." A terrible battle erupted. "The Indians," it was reported, "with arrows and spears with points made of sharpened bone or fish spines wounded two Castilians." Such ferocity had not been expected. The entire landing party was in danger. Their rather surprised leader promptly ordered a retreat. Even though he had seen his share of battles, Ponce de León thought it best to leave. In the end, "Juan Ponce collected his men, and they departed for the night."[29]

HOME AGAIN

Battered and bloody, Ponce de León's sailors were more than happy to go. Back on board, they raised the sails and floated off. Luckily, as they continued their travels, the expedition came across friendlier Indians. The crews traded with these villages and even took one Indian aboard as a guide and interpreter. Yet despite all the trading and fighting, none of the men forgot why they had sailed north in the first place. Every time they talked to the local people, they asked about gold. The Indians, for their part, always answered the same way: they did not know anything about it. Some Indians claimed to have heard tales of great riches in other places, but not near their villages. No gold around here was the standard reply. Of course, a few villagers did mention something about a fountain or pond flowing with miraculous waters. It was rumored that these waters could heal the sick and restore youth to the elderly. But as for gold–nothing.

Ponce de León did not give up. He was sure that the treasure trove he sought had to be around somewhere. Every place he stopped, he quizzed the inhabitants. None of them were of any help. Riches had to be lying about somewhere, he told himself. Finally, Ponce de León decided that with winter coming, it was a good idea to leave. The gold would have to wait. The disappointed explorer refitted and resupplied his ships, and made for home. His journey back was uneventful. On October 19, 1513, his fleet dropped anchor in the main harbor of San Juan Bautista, newly renamed as Puerto Rico.

Ponce de León made the most of his trip as he recounted his exploits. He thrilled his audiences. He told tantalizing stories about the fierce Indians, the elusive gold, and the mysterious fountain that made the old young again. People listened intently, especially when the explorer spoke of the fountain "that turned men from old men to boys."[30] Even in the sixteenth century, people had longed to restore their youth. The tale of the magic fountain, therefore,

This illustration shows Ponce de León searching for the Fountain of Youth during his 1513 expedition to Florida. When Ponce de León returned to Puerto Rico, many were intrigued by the stories of a mysterious fountain that made the old young again.

really got their attention. So, despite his failure in finding the riches he sought, Ponce de León returned to Puerto Rico triumphant. More important, he came back home as the discoverer and master of Florida.

Test Your Knowledge

1 How did King Ferdinand respond to Ponce de León's request to explore the lands north of Cuba?

   a. He told Ponce de León that those lands were already promised to Diego Columbus.

   b. Ferdinand told Ponce de León he must share any wealth he found with Diego Columbus.

   c. Ferdinand not only granted Ponce de León permission to explore the lands, but also to govern them and keep any wealth he found.

   d. None of the above.

2 Ponce de León's ships on the Florida expedition included

   a. the *Nina*.

   b. the *Santiago*.

   c. the *Isabella*.

   d. all of the above.

3 Why did Ponce de León bring plenty of paper on his voyage?

   a. He hoped to map his entire route for future reference.

   b. He hoped to print his own money in the new country he established.

   c. He hoped to write a book about his experiences.

   d. None of the above.

4 How was Ponce de León's first Florida landing
party received by the local Indians?

   a. The Indians welcomed the new visitors
immediately.

   b. The Indians were eager to establish trade with
Ponce de León's ships.

   c. The Indians were hostile and battled Ponce
de León's men.

   d. None of the above.

5 How much gold did Ponce de León's first trip to
Florida yield?

   a. The equivalent of 1,000 gold doubloons

   b. The equivalent of 100 gold bars

   c. A few gold items, including a ceremonial mask

   d. No gold at all

ANSWERS: 1. c; 2. b; 3. a; 4. c; 5. d

Building on Success

Ponce de León was now wealthy and famous. Most men would have been quite content at this point, but not Ponce de León. He refused to rest on his success. Now, as he had already learned, was the time to be extra vigilant. The explorer was determined to make sure he kept what he had worked so hard to get. Ponce de León wanted to guarantee that no one challenged his authority over Florida. Despite Ferdinand's earlier assurances, Ponce de León remembered well how Diego Columbus had forced him out of office in Puerto Rico. He did not want that to happen again. Ponce de León did not intend to take any chances. He requested a private audience with the king himself, and then sailed for Spain in April 1514.

On the long crossing, he had time to think. He had no idea what kind of reception to expect. Maybe the king would be angry. Perhaps the adventurer had enemies at the royal court he did not know about. His position might not be as strong as he thought. Such concerns spun in his head. Then he reminded himself about the slight precaution he had taken. That helped ease his worry. Before leaving Hispaniola, he had packed 5,000 gold pieces with his luggage. Money might help smooth the way, he hoped, just in case there was any trouble.

TALKING TO THE KING

It took a little over three weeks to make the Atlantic crossing. After dropping anchor in the port of Bayona, Ponce de León went directly to the king.

Ferdinand, at that moment, was holding court in the city of Valladolid. Anyone who visited the king had to be just a bit nervous about what his mood would be. An angry or disappointed king could be dangerous. Luckily for him, Ponce de León caught Ferdinand in a very good mood. The explorer received a warm and truly royal greeting. Ferdinand had always liked Ponce de León. The king admired his courage, determination, and sense of adventure. The king loved tales of exploration and conquest, and he hoped to hear some really good stories from Ponce de León. More important, though, Ferdinand trusted Ponce de León. Many royal officials openly abused the power that the king had granted them. Greed and corruption were commonplace in early Spain. Men stole from the royal treasury, lied in official reports, and used government positions for personal profit. But not Ponce de León. He certainly defended his own interests, but he did so honestly and in plain view, for everyone to see. The king appreciated that.

Ferdinand felt so confident in Ponce de León's loyalty that he showered him with titles and privileges. The king gave Ponce de León broad new powers. In September 1514, Ferdinand signed papers that gave control of Florida and all the islands near it to one man, Ponce de León. That was everything Ponce de León had wished for, but Ferdinand went further. Shocking everybody at the royal court, the king also dubbed the explorer a knight. The once obscure boy from a little village was suddenly transformed into Sir John—Don Juan Ponce de León.

As a knight, royal governor, and favorite of the king, Ponce de León was expected to serve not only himself but the entire kingdom. He became Ferdinand's personal representative. Ponce de León, when he returned to the New World, would be very busy. Topping his list of tasks was the implementation of a new royal edict, the *Requerimiento*, the Requirement. The *Requerimiento* was basically an order issued to the Indians that forced them to obey Ferdinand and his officials. It had to be read to every Indian tribe encountered to give the natives a chance to comply peacefully, even though they could not understand Spanish and the message was often read far away from them. The penalty for disobedience was death. Ferdinand commanded that the American Indians submit to Spanish rule. They also had to accept Christianity and the authority of the Catholic Church. The *Requerimiento* ordered the Indians to "acknowledge the Church as the Ruler and Superior of the whole world."[31] They were told to obey Catholic missionaries and listen to the word of the Spanish God—or else.

The edict promised the Indians that if they did what they "are obliged to do," they could expect "all love and charity" in return. The king guaranteed their future safety: "you, your wives, and your children [will be] free without servitude." In fact, Ferdinand pledged to give the Indians "many privileges and exceptions . . . many benefits." All they had to do was follow Spanish orders. "But if you do not do this," the *Requerimiento* warned, "we shall powerfully enter into your country." The Spanish threatened to attack the Indians and "take you and your wives and your children and make slaves of them."[32] No disobedience would be tolerated.

The *Requerimiento* was the king's final word. The Indians of the New World were his subjects now, and they would act like it. All of Ferdinand's officials, including Ponce de León, were expected to enforce

When Charles I, above, became the new king of Spain, Ponce de León decided he had to return to Spain. He wanted to make sure that Charles honored the agreements he had made with the previous king, Ferdinand.

the decree. Ponce de León was directly charged with seeing to it that the Indians in his territory conformed. By "every way and means that you can devise," the king commanded Ponce de León, "you are to bring [the Indians] to understand our Catholic Faith, and to obey and serve it as they are obliged to."[33] Ponce de León was given total authority to accomplish his mission. Even his old enemy Diego Columbus had to stand aside. King Ferdinand specifically told Columbus not to interfere with Ponce de León. The king wrote to Ponce de León telling him that he had commanded "Don Diego Columbus [to give] you all of the favor and assistance you might need, without impeding you in any manner whatsoever."[34]

PUTTING THE KING'S WORDS INTO ACTION

With all of his new powers and privileges, Ponce de León sailed back to the New World in May 1515. He had with him a fleet of three ships carrying 150 armed men. The hope was to impress the Indians with Spanish might. Show them some steel, Ponce de León thought, and the Indians would fall into line. If they did not do as the king had commanded, they would face Spanish guns. Resistance would not be tolerated. Ponce de León would make the Indians obey, or he would kill them. He did not hate them, but no one was allowed to defy the crown.

Ponce de León, in a strange way, actually looked forward to the adventure of it all. A good fight did not scare him. Anyway, the Indians were unlikely to take on him and his men. Or so Ponce de León imagined. When he finally arrived in the Caribbean, however, he found a vastly different situation. He discovered that the Indians who lived on the Caribbean islands had no intention of giving in. The would-be conqueror met up with a people determined to remain free. The Indians had heard of the *Requerimiento*, and refused to comply. They chose to resist.

True to his word, Ponce de León set about forcing them to obey the orders of a king they had never known. Ponce de León admired their courage, but he was determined to force the Indians' submission. He sent soldiers to attack them. The troops were harshly received. Everywhere the islanders fought fiercely. Village after village challenged the Spanish. No matter where Ponce de León and his troops went they met with arrows and spears. Despite superior weapons, Ponce de León and his men had to retreat. The commander reluctantly gave up on this particular attempt to subdue the Indians. Frustrated, he fell back to Puerto Rico to regroup.

Ponce de León wasted no time in coming up with a new strategy against the Indians. But before he could take them on again, bad news arrived. Word got to him that his powerful ally and friend, Ferdinand, had died. The new king was his grandson, Charles I. Fearing that Charles might not honor the agreements made by Ferdinand, Ponce de León decided that it would be a good idea to return to Spain once more. He had to make sure that Charles would not take away everything he had worked so hard to get.

A NEW KING, A NEW MISSION

Time was short. Ponce de León took the fastest ship he could find, and headed out to sea. He arrived in Castile in November 1516—and stayed there for the next two years. It took Ponce de León that long to guarantee his political position. He worked tirelessly to protect his privileges and possessions in the New

World. He was successful, in the end, but two years was a long time to be away. By the time he returned to the islands, Ponce de León discovered that attention had shifted away from Florida. Nobody was paying much attention to it anymore. The effort to enforce the *Requerimiento* was old news. The talk now was all about Mexico, gold, and Ponce de León's friend, Hernán Cortés. Cortés was doing more than just forcing a bunch of villagers to behave. He was about to conquer an empire.

Ponce de León was acquainted with most, if not all, of the Spanish adventurers in the Caribbean in the early sixteenth century. Vasco Núñez de Balboa, the man who first laid eyes on the Pacific Ocean, was a close friend; he also knew Cortés very well. Ponce de León was aware that Cortés was an ambitious man determined to grab the riches of Mexico for himself and, of course, Spain. Cortés wanted all the Aztec gold he could carry away. In 1519, he made his move. Cortés landed in Mexico with 600 men and began his conquest of the Aztecs.

People on both sides of the Atlantic, for the next two years, followed Cortés's exploits. They watched as he brought down perhaps the largest and strongest kingdom that pre-Columbian America had ever seen. No one matched the Aztecs in power and wealth. Now, it all belonged to Cortés and the crown. Those not interested in Mexico could always watch the drama of Ferdinand Magellan's daring attempt to sail around the world under a Spanish flag. And there were others. No matter where Ponce

A Spanish Bride

While the result of Ponce de León's travels to Spain is clear, some parts of his trip remain hazy. The visit was no social call. He was there to see the new king, Charles I. His old friend, King Ferdinand, had died just months before, and Ponce de León had to make sure that Charles would let him keep his property and titles in the New World.

But perhaps the trip was not all business either. Ponce de León was a loyal servant of the king, but he was also a man. Some stories say that Ponce de León's loving wife, Leonor, died while he was in Spain; no one knew how she died. And one account of his time in Spain says that he met a beautiful young girl named Juana de Pineda. She was so de León looked, men were upstaging him. Fame and money were elsewhere. Florida seemed like a backwater now. Ponce de León and his designs on Florida were ignored.

There was, to be sure, still a little bit of interest in Florida but nothing like before. Ponce de León could almost feel the historical moment slipping

charming and witty that Ponce de León soon fell in love with her. He asked Juana to marry him right then and there. She felt strongly about Ponce de León, too; Juana said yes. Ponce de León had a new wife.

Or, maybe not. There is no record of Leonor dying until long after Ponce de León came home from Spain. Nor is there any solid evidence for any marriage to a girl named Juana. In truth, no one knows what really happened on that second trip to Spain. The visit is shrouded in mystery. The only sure thing is that Ponce de León got permission to go back to Florida one more time. It would be his last voyage.

An Aztec Indian cultivates corn in Mexico. Ponce de León's compatriot, Hernán Cortés, landed in Mexico in 1519 and took two years to conquer the mighty Aztec Empire and capture its gold. Ponce de León, meanwhile, looked north toward Florida to gain his riches.

away. Soon no one would care about him or his Florida. So, in 1521, he decided to make another trip north. This time Ponce de León did not just want to explore and make bold claims as he had before. This go-around, he intended to conquer, colonize, and stay.

Test Your Knowledge

1 How was Ponce de León received by King Ferdinand at Valladolid?

   a. Ferdinand viewed Ponce de León as a failure because he had found no gold.

   b. Ferdinand insisted that Ponce de León step aside in favor of Diego Columbus.

   c. Ferdinand greeted Ponce de León as a hero, giving him titles and privileges.

   d. None of the above.

2 What was the *Requerimiento*?

   a. A royal order forcing the Indians to bow to the will of King Ferdinand.

   b. A document that Ferdinand insisted be read to all native peoples whom Ponce de León encountered.

   c. A royal order declaring that the Indians adopt the Catholic faith.

   d. All of the above.

3 What became of the *Requerimiento* when King Ferdinand died?

   a. It was forgotten for a time.

   b. It was upheld by the new king, Charles I.

   c. It was officially revoked by the new king.

   d. It succeeded in converting the Aztecs to Catholicism.

4 What event overshadowed Ponce de León's
Florida expedition?
a. A devastating earthquake in Spain
b. Discovery of an all-sea route to the Pacific
c. Cortés and his conquest of the Aztecs
d. None of the above

5 What were Ponce de León's plans for his return
to the Americas?
a. To bring back even more gold than Cortés
b. To conquer the Indians, colonize the land,
and stay
c. To convert all the Indians to Catholicism
d. To kill Cortés

Florida and the Price of Ambition

Ponce de León outlined his plans for another trip to Florida in a letter to King Charles. He told Charles, in February 1521, that it had always been his "habit and custom . . . to serve . . . the Royal Crown" in the New World. The adventurer contended that he had faithfully followed every order issued by Ferdinand, and hoped "to continue in the service of Your Majesty." Ponce de León made clear his devotion. He did so with very carefully chosen words. He did not know the new king as well as the old one. Charles was not Ferdinand. Ponce de León was not sure how easily he could be offended. One small slip-up, and Ponce de León might lose his influence and power. So, he said over and over how loyal he was. Then, he gently reminded the monarch how he had "discovered at my expense . . . the Florida Island and others in its region."[35]

After this cautious introduction, Ponce de León got down to the real business at hand. "I am returning to [Florida]," he proudly announced, "to settle it." The expedition would be very different from the first one, he promised. His proposed return trip would represent a serious effort to spread "the name of Jesus Christ," and develop "the agricultural production of that land."[36] Such a bold effort would be neither easy nor inexpensive. Ponce de León hinted strongly in his letter that he hoped the king might pick up all, or at least most, of the tab. "Up until now I have not asked for favors," the explorer wrote. But that was about to change. He wanted the crown to help finance his Florida journey. Much to his surprise, Charles readily agreed. The king gave his approval for another try at settling Florida. Ten days after receiving approval in writing, Ponce de León sailed from Puerto Rico at the head of "another armed fleet." He went out determined "to settle the Florida Island, and make discoveries in the neighboring regions."[37]

FLORIDA—ONE MORE TIME

One of the "discoveries" many people, at least those still paying attention, prayed that Ponce de León would make was that of the fabled Fountain of Youth. Most colonists in the Caribbean already knew by 1521 that no such fountain existed. Yet rumors persistently swirled about a miraculous spring. It was said to be somewhere in the northern islands, exactly where Ponce de León was returning. Coming across a fountain that made old people young again would be a real prize. It probably would never be found, but there was no harm in looking. The evidence, however, suggests that Ponce de León did not look too hard. Other people might have been interested in it, but he was not.

A painting depicts Ponce de León being given water from the fabled Fountain of Youth. Though Ponce de León is famously associated with the Fountain of Youth, most evidence suggests that the explorer did not search too hard to find it.

It appears, in fact, that the Fountain of Youth, which he is famously associated with, was never one of Ponce de León's objectives. What he sought above all else was gold, followed very closely by land and political power. Ponce de León could not care less if Florida made him young, as long as it made him rich and famous.

Hopeful and well prepared, Ponce de León sailed northward once more in 1521. His "fleet" was composed of two strong ships carrying 200 men and 50 horses. The men were equipped for war, if need be. They brought state-of-the-art weaponry. These colonists could and would fight. But fighting was not living. The men who accompanied Ponce de León looked well beyond battle. Along with swords and armor, the ships' holds contained goats, pigs, sheep, and cattle. The expedition had everything it needed to start farming as soon as it arrived. Each vessel was packed with bags full of seeds, and men who hoped to grow them into crops.

Ponce de León thought about all the weapons and equipment, and was reassured. Oddly, he expected an easy time ahead. His memory was painfully short. Despite his earlier encounters with angry locals, he anticipated neither a hostile environment nor a hostile reception. The overly confident explorer got both. First, he underestimated the climate. The weather turned chilly in Florida during the winter, especially in the northern parts. That is where his expedition planned to land. Also, the soil was far less suited to farming than Ponce de

León had imagined. Even if he had successfully planted a colony in Florida, it probably would not have lasted long. In addition, the local Indians welcomed intruders even less than the ones the explorer had previously met. They wanted nothing to do with strangers, particularly Spanish ones. They had heard stories about Spanish cruelty. They were ready to defend their homes and their land against anyone. In their favor, the Indians had the weapons and numbers to do so effectively. The arms and men Ponce de León brought along would not be enough.

According to a later writer, Florida's weather "was very disagreeable and different from what [Ponce de León] had imagined." The Indians ended up being "very savage and bellicose and furious and uncontrollable . . . ." Unaware of all this, Ponce de León prepared "as if the business of his settlement was no more than arriving and cultivating the land and grazing his livestock."[38]

PAYING THE PRICE FOR FLORIDA

Properly prepared or not, Ponce de León's miniature armada crashed through the waves toward

In his mission to Florida in 1521, Ponce de León hoped to establish a settlement and grow crops, possibly like the sugarcane shown here. He and his men, however, found the soil much less suited to farming than they had imagined.

Florida. No one is sure precisely where the Spanish ships first made landfall. The best guess is somewhere along the western coast, perhaps near modern-day Tampa Bay. What is known is that the men immediately began building a settlement. Just as quickly, they were attacked. The stories about the Indians' ferocity and their willingness to resist Spanish rule turned out to be true.

The Indians were indeed "very surely" not willing "to easily give up their liberty."[39] They also knew quite well that the Spanish meant them no good. Wherever the Spanish went, they stole Indian land. This time would be no different, so the native people chose to fight. They resisted every effort at negotiation. They refused to even consider submitting to the Spanish. They rejected the mere idea of becoming Christians.

Periodic fighting flared through the spring of 1521. By the summer, tensions were high and hatred ran deep. At last, the Indians launched a major assault. A large force of warriors hit Ponce de León's main settlement. The Spanish held the technological edge in the battle, but the Indians were more numerous and well motivated. The Spanish had metal armor, horses, and firearms. But these Indians, unlike the Tainos before, carried powerful bows and lethal arrows. Some warriors were deadly marksmen. Most were capable of putting an arrow, often tipped with a shark's tooth or stingray spine, between the metal plates of a Spaniard's armor. Shots like that meant instant death. Indian bows, additionally, fired much faster than their enemies' cumbersome matchlock muskets. Matchlocks were hard to load, difficult to aim, and prone to misfiring. Once the Indians got used to the smoke and noise of a musket's discharge, they lost

Going Home for the Last Time

Ponce de León is one of the best-known explorers in American history. He is remembered as one of a group of men who, for better or worse, gave Spain its New World empire. Even people who know little about history have heard of Ponce de León. They hear his name and immediately think of Florida or, more often, the fabled Fountain of Youth. But in his own time, he was pretty much ignored.

When he died, few people noted it. It was as if Don Juan Ponce de León had been just a common adventurer. Never mind all that he had done for Spain. People forgot that he had fought valiantly for his homeland in Europe and the Americas. He established the first colony on their fear of it. Taken together, the Indians held the edge, and they used it.

The attack on the Spanish settlement became a rout. As the Indians charged in, the Spanish soldiers fell all over the place. Firing as best they could, the men dropped back and were very soon in full retreat. The tiny outpost was overrun. Ponce de

the island of Puerto Rico, and he discovered Florida. Histories of the New World written in the sixteenth century barely mention him. His life was brushed aside.

Nor was much care given to Ponce de León after he died in 1521. He was buried quickly, and without much fuss, on the island of Cuba, at Havana. Even though he had spent many years of his life in Puerto Rico and had his home there, nobody thought to send him back. It took 38 years for someone to give Ponce de León a chance to go home. His remains did not arrive back in San Juan until 1559. Ponce de León, in life, wandered all over the Caribbean. Today he rests peacefully— at home.

León was one of the casualties dragged away by the retreating troops. An arrow had torn into his leg, cutting a major artery. He was bleeding to death. His men rushed him to the ships and tried to stop the bleeding. They did well enough, and soon the entire force was heading out toward Cuba, and safety. Along the way, the men worked feverishly to keep Ponce de León alive.

The ships, under full sail, raced for Cuba. One ship's captain thought Mexico was closer, so he headed there. The vessel carrying Ponce de León stayed on course. It soon reached Havana, where it became clear that Ponce de León would not make it. He had lost too much blood, despite his soldiers' best efforts. A local doctor went to work on the explorer, but he had no better luck. There was nothing else anyone could do. Not long after arriving in Cuba, Ponce de León died. With him went his dreams of gold and fame—and Florida.

Test Your Knowledge

1 How did King Charles I react to Ponce de León's plan to return to Florida?

   a. Charles approved and agreed to fund the expedition.

   b. Charles approved, but insisted that Ponce de León fund the expedition.

   c. Charles wanted nothing to do with Florida and forbade Ponce de León to go.

   d. None of the above.

2 How was Ponce de León's second expedition to Florida equipped?

   a. With 200 well-armed men and 50 horses

   b. With only primitive weapons and a few farm tools

   c. With jewelry and gold to trade with the Indians

   d. None of the above

3 What factors had Ponce de León not anticipated in his return to Florida?

   a. The chilly winter climate of northern Florida

   b. The hostility of the local Indians

   c. The poor nature of the soil for farming

   d. All of the above

4 How important was it for Ponce de León to find the Fountain of Youth?

a. It was his main goal, and he exhausted his supplies in his search.

b. It was relatively unimportant, and he spent little time searching for it.

c. It was more important than establishing a permanent settlement.

d. None of the above.

5 How did Juan Ponce de León die?

a. He contracted malaria while in Florida.

b. He was killed by his own men after failing to find the Fountain of Youth.

c. He was shot in the leg by an Indian's arrow and bled slowly to death.

d. None of the above.

ANSWERS: 1. a; 2. a; 3. d; 4. b; 5. c

Ponce de León, the New World, and History

Excitement, adventure, danger—Ponce de León's story would be worth telling even if he had never become famous. Following him on his many journeys, through his many ups and downs, makes for great reading. Whatever the final outcome of his life's work, the story is thrilling. Yet the real value of learning about this intrepid explorer lies in what can be learned about much larger things. Ponce de León is like a mirror in which we can see reflections not only of his time, but also our own. In him, we can see the whole process of building the Spanish Empire. We can also see more clearly how Europe in general tried to conquer the New World. Lastly, we can see our own vision of history reflected back to us. Looking at Ponce de León, we can learn why we see him, and the rest of history, the way we do. Ponce de León, then, is not only a famous figure, but a fine resource as well.

Ponce de León was never a heroic character, just a man. But there is no denying that he did do some extraordinary things. His determination and drive made the explorer stand out from those around him. It must be remembered, however, that Ponce de León was just one small part of a much bigger process of Spanish colonization. There was a whole world of change swirling around him. There was conflict, too. Spain was taking over the New World, and struggling with the Native Americans along the way. This was happening from Mexico to South America, and all

A statue of Ponce de León adorns the streets of Old San Juan, Puerto Rico. In a quest to find gold, Ponce de León settled the island of Puerto Rico, which was then called San Juan Bautista.

the way up into what is today the United States. Ponce de León and his experiences were part of this. He reflected perfectly the basic character of Spain's colonial program. Gold drew the Spanish into the New World and stimulated the desire for adventure. That led to an urge to conquer, settle, and govern lands that did not belong to them. This, in turn, gave rise to an entire imperial structure based on taking what the New World had to offer and using it for Spanish gain. This was Spanish America; this was Ponce de León.

Driven by faith, greed, and the urge to explore, the Spanish sailed west to the Americas. Many men, just like Ponce de León, hoped to earn fame and fortune while serving their king and God. They looked out for themselves first, but worked tirelessly for Spain. Whole groups of settlers, of course, came to the Caribbean and Mexico from Spain. Towns, cities, and colonies were set up pretty quickly. But individual men, like Ponce de León, were the engines that powered that settlement. The Spanish Empire in the Americas, in fact, rose up on the shoulders of men like Columbus, Balboa, Cortés, and Ponce de León. So, if someone wanted to write a "typical" story of Spanish conquest, they could easily use Ponce de León's as a model. Exploration, to find gold and grab land from the Indians, followed by settlement, was exactly what Ponce de León did. In this he was thoroughly Spanish. If we learn his story, then, we learn for the most part the bigger one of Spain in the New World.

Yet what about motivation, the wants and needs that made all of this happen? Ponce de León loved adventure, but he hungered for gold. His obsession with the yellow metal mirrored similar desires in thousands of European hearts, and not just Spanish ones. Even for the French and the English, wealth motivated most of the early colonists in the New World. The Spanish tried to dig up as much gold as they could. But the French found their fortune in the fur trade. The first French settlers in North America craved the easy money that came from the fur of beavers, foxes, and other animals. The English, famous for their religious goals, also wanted to make money in the New World. English merchants, traders, and businessmen hoped to make a fortune on timber, sugar, and tobacco. In short, Europeans wanted to get rich in America, just like Ponce de León. The basic elements of his life were repeated over and over again, all over North and South America.

Europe longed for the treasures hidden in the Americas, as did Ponce de León. His ultimate goal in all of his efforts was to get as much wealth and power as possible. Everything else flowed from that. He was not unique, though, in this. Europeans in general came to the New World for the same reasons, at least in the beginning. So Ponce de León was an example not only of the Spanish model of conquest, but also of the overall European drive to settle and exploit the Americas. Ponce de León's tale is that of an entire generation, of whole cultures on the move.

Finally, Ponce de León's exploits, and those of the many men like him, helped to craft the focus of American history and identity. From its earliest days, the writing of American history has centered on individual accomplishments. Generations of students have been taught to put the individual front and center in the historical process. To be sure, the concentration on "great men" has

Ponce de León's feats, real and imagined, are still conjured up in the names of towns and places in Florida and the Caribbean. Here, a sign in St. Augustine, Florida, points to the supposed Fountain of Youth.

changed into a more useful and more accurate study of "great people." Women, black Americans, and a host of others are no longer excluded from the American story. And yet, even when these groups are included and discussed, it is almost always in individual terms. Modern Americans

Names and Places

Americans might not know much about the details of Ponce de León's life, but they can never forget his name. Students hear it in classrooms around the country and write reports on his adventures. History textbooks almost always give him some space in their pages. But maps give Ponce de León his best popular exposure. His accomplishments are often ignored; his name, however, is repeated over and over again in the brightly colored guides to cities and towns in Puerto Rico and Florida.

Puerto Rico, as you would expect, is filled with places named for the great explorer. A major street in Puerto Rico's capital, San Juan, is named continue to assume that history is driven by this or that person who did something special. Americans, in other words, persist in thinking of hi*story* as a personal *story*.

History, Americans believe, is a record of brave men and women making it on their own. Personal

Avenida Ponce de León. The island's second largest city is called Ponce.

Yet Juan Ponce de León pops up in Florida like nowhere else. The state capital, Tallahassee, is in León County. Streets, schools, even entertainment centers carry his name. The city of St. Augustine, for example, has a Ponce de León Golf and Conference Center. The signs identifying several towns and waterways in the state also recall Ponce de León's role in Florida's history. No matter where you go in Florida, somewhere you will find a little reminder of the man who found the place and claimed it for Spain. His memory connects modern Floridians, indeed all Americans, to their past, and to themselves.

courage and independence are what really count. Those are the qualities that cause change and growth. Famous people seem to push the world along in time. With thinking like this, it is no surprise that Americans have a reputation for being fiercely individualistic. Much more so than people in other countries, Americans find inspiration in stories about boldness and risk-taking by individual men and women. So they look for those qualities in their historical characters, and in themselves. When one thinks about it in this way, Ponce de León is very American.

The fascinating tale of Ponce de León's struggles and discoveries highlights many areas of the American experience. It is more than simply a good adventure story, although it is that, too. Ponce de León tells us about who people used to be, and who they are today. The enchanted fountain that supposedly made old men young again promised long life. Ponce de León's half-hearted search for it has become a legend even in failure. But in a certain way he succeeded after all. Through the story of his life, Ponce de León discovered a way to remain fresh and new for generations of Americans.

No one will ever forget the young Castilian squire who discovered Florida and became the Ponce de León we remember today.

Test Your Knowledge

1 Why did the Spanish sail west to the Americas?
   a. To search for gold and riches
   b. To spread the Catholic faith
   c. Out of a general sense of adventure
   d. All of the above

2 In contrast to the Spanish, the French found their American fortunes in
   a. coal and diamonds.
   b. the fur trade.
   c. lumber and sawmills.
   d. none of the above.

3 How did Ponce de León's accomplishments mirror those of Spain?
   a. Both sought to defeat the French.
   b. Both sought to advance the cause of science.
   c. Both sought to gain wealth and prestige.
   d. None of the above.

4 In what way do Americans often view history?
   a. As a series of interconnected events
   b. As the complex stories of many minor players
   c. As pivotal moves by a select few powerful individuals
   d. None of the above

5 For which of the following is Ponce de León perhaps best remembered?

a. The legend of his search for the Fountain of Youth

b. His military loss against the Indians

c. His discovery of Florida

d. None of the above

ANSWERS: 1. d; 2. b; 3. c; 4. c; 5. a

1474 (?) Juan Ponce de León is born (though several historians believe he may have been born as early as 1460).

1492 After centuries of warfare, the armies of Christian Spain drive out the Muslims who had been on the Iberian Peninsula since 711. Christopher Columbus leaves on his famous voyage the same year.

1493 Ponce de León sees the New World for the first time when he goes with Columbus on his second trip to America.

1502 Ponce de León returns to the Caribbean, and settles on the island of Hispaniola. He takes part

1474 (?) Juan Ponce de León is born.

1493 Ponce de León sees the New World for the first time when he goes with Columbus on his second trip to America.

1509 King Ferdinand makes Ponce de León the governor of Puerto Rico. The move infuriates Christopher Columbus's son, Diego, and leads to two years of disagreement.

1474

1502 Ponce de León returns to the Caribbean, and settles on Hispaniola. He helps put down an uprising, and is rewarded with land.

1508 After an earlier secret trip, Ponce de León makes an official journey to Puerto Rico.

in putting down an uprising on the island by the Taino Indians, and is rewarded with land.

1508 After an earlier secret trip, Ponce de León makes an official journey to the island of Puerto Rico.

1509 King Ferdinand makes Ponce de León the governor of Puerto Rico. The move infuriates Christopher Columbus's son, Diego, and leads to two years of disagreement.

1511 A lawsuit, brought by Diego Columbus, is settled by the Spanish royal council in his favor. Ponce de León is forced to give up his governorship.

1511 A lawsuit, brought by Diego Columbus, is settled in his favor. Ponce de León is forced to give up his governorship.

1516 Ponce de León travels back to Spain to meet the new king, Charles I, and guarantee his political position in the New World.

1521

1513 Ponce de León makes his first trip to Florida.

1521 Ponce de León returns to Florida. He dies from an arrow wound received in battle with the Indians.

1513 Ponce de León makes his first trip to Florida.

1516 King Ferdinand dies. Ponce de León travels back to Spain to meet the new king, Charles I, and guarantee his political position in the New World. He stays in Spain for two years.

1521 Ponce de León returns to Florida to set up a permanent settlement. He dies from an arrow wound received in battle with the Florida Indians.

Chapter 1
1493

1. Paolo Emilio Taviani, *Columbus: The Great Adventure, His Life, His Times, and His Voyages* (New York: Orion Books, 1991), 144.

2. Björn Landström, *Columbus: The Story of Don Cristóbal Colón, Admiral of the Ocean Sea, and His Four Voyages Westward to the Indies* (New York: The Macmillan Company, 1966), 112.

3. Ibid., 108.

Chapter 2
A New Spain and a New World

4. J.M. Roberts, *A History of Europe* (New York: Allen Lane, 1996), 100.

5. Ibid., 120.

6. Edward Potts Cheyney, *European Background of American History, 1300–1600* (New York: Frederick Ungar Publishing Company, 1966), 39.

7. J.H. Elliott, *Imperial Spain, 1469–1716* (New York: Penguin Books, 1963), 24.

8. Taviani, *Columbus*, 82.

9. Landström, *Columbus*, 44.

10. Ibid., 106.

Chapter 3
A Young Adventurer

11. Douglas T. Peck, *Ponce de León and the Discovery of Florida: The Man, The Myth, and The Truth* (Pogo Press, 1993), 3.

12. Kenneth R. Scholberg, *Spanish Life in the Late Middle Ages* (Chapel Hill, NC: University of North Carolina Press, 1965), 85.

13. Ibid., 80–81.

14. Robert Fuson, *Juan Ponce de León and the Spanish Discovery of Puerto Rico and Florida* (Blacksburg, VA: The McDonald & Woodward Publishing Company, 2000), 39.

15. Peck, *Ponce de León*, 3.

16. James Axtell, *Beyond 1492: Encounters in Colonial North America* (New York: Oxford University Press, 1992), 300.

17. Fuson, *Juan Ponce*, 64.

Chapter 4
A New Life in a New Land

18. Washington Irving, *The Voyages and Discoveries of the Companions of Columbus* (1831; reprint, New York: Frederick Ungar Publishing Company, 1960), 323.

19. Fuson, *Juan Ponce*, 72.

20. Ibid., 80.

21. Peck, *Ponce de León*, 9.

Chapter 5
Finding Florida

22. Fuson, *Juan Ponce*, 89.

23. Ibid., 92

24. Ibid., 93.

25. Ibid.

26. Ibid., 95.

27. Peck, *Ponce de León*, 40

28. Fuson, *Juan Ponce*, 106.

29. Ibid.

30. Ibid., 114.

Chapter 6
Building on Success

31. Fuson, *Juan Ponce*, 135.

32. Ibid.

33. Ibid., 130.

34. Ibid., 131.

Chapter 7
Florida and the Price of Ambition

35. Fuson, *Juan Ponce*, 162.

36. Ibid., 162-163.

37. Ibid., 163.

38. Ibid., 165.

39. Ibid.

Axtell, James. *Beyond 1492: Encounters in Colonial North America.* New York: Oxford University Press, 1992.

Cheyney, Edward Potts. *European Background of American History, 1300–1600.* New York: Frederick Ungar Publishing Company, 1966.

Elliott, J.H. *Imperial Spain, 1469–1716.* New York: Penguin Books, 1963.

———. *The Old World and the New, 1492–1650.* New York: Cambridge University Press, 1970.

Fuson, Robert. *Juan Ponce de León and the Spanish Discovery of Puerto Rico and Florida.* Blacksburg, VA: The McDonald & Woodward Publishing Company, 2000.

Irving, Washington. *The Voyages and Discoveries of the Companions of Columbus.* 1831, reprint; New York: Frederick Ungar Publishing Company, 1960.

Landström, Björn. *Columbus: The Story of Don Cristóbal Colón, Admiral of the Ocean Sea, and His Four Voyages Westward to the Indies.* New York: The Macmillan Company, 1966.

Peck, Douglas T. *Ponce de León and the Discovery of Florida: The Man, The Myth, and The Truth.* Pogo Press, 1993.

Roberts, J.M. *A History of Europe.* New York: Allen Lane, 1996.

Taviani, Paolo Emilio. *Columbus: The Great Adventure, His Life, His Times, and His Voyages.* New York: Orion Books, 1991.

Books

Blassingame, Wyatt. *Ponce de León.* Broomall, PA: Chelsea House Publishers, 1991.

Heinrichs, Ann. *Ponce de León: Ponce de León Searches for the Fountain of Youth.* Minneapolis, MN: Compass Point Books, 2002.

Molzahn, Arlene Bourgeois. *Ponce de Leon: Explorer of Florida.* Berkeley Heights, NJ: Enslow Publishers, 2003.

Websites

Who was Ponce de León?
http://www.publicbookshelf.org/public_html/Our_Country_Vol_1/whowaspo_bf.html

Ponce de León and the Fountain of Youth
http://www.socialstudiesforkids.com/articles/worldhistory/juanponcedeleon1.htm

Ponce de León
http://multimedia.esuhsd.org/2000/ed_project/135_web/studentprojects/ageexploration/poncedeleon.html

Juan Ponce de León
http://www.fcps.k12.va.us/KingsParkES/technology/bios/deleon.htm

John C. Davenport holds a Ph.D. from the University of Connecticut and currently teaches at Corte Madera School in Portola Valley, California. Davenport is the author of several other books, including biographies of the Muslim leader Saladin and the writer C.S. Lewis. He lives in San Carlos, California, with his wife, Jennifer, and his two sons, William and Andrew.

William H. Goetzmann is the Jack S. Blanton, Sr. Chair in History and American Studies at the University of Texas, Austin. Dr. Goetzmann was awarded the Joseph Pulitzer and Francis Parkman Prizes for American History, 1967, for *Exploration and Empire: The Explorer and the Scientist in the Winning of the American West.* In 1999, he was elected a member of the American Philosophical Society, founded by Benjamin Franklin in 1743, to honor achievement in the sciences and humanities.